D0167426

Clashing Symbols

Also by Michael Paul Gallagher

The Human Poetry of Faith
Free to Believe
Letters on Prayer
Where is Your God?
What Are They Saying About Unbelief?

Clashing Symbols

An Introduction to Faith and Culture

NEW AND REVISED EDITION

MICHAEL PAUL GALLAGHER, s.j.

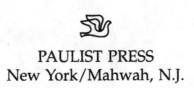

PAULIST PRESS
New York/Mahwah, N.J.

Published in the United States in 2003
Paulist Press
997 Macarthur Boulevard
Mahwah, N.J. 07430

First published in Great Britain in 1997
Darton, Longman and Todd Ltd
1 Spencer Court
140–142 Wandsworth High Street
London SW18 4JJ

This revised and expanded edition 2003

ISBN 0-8091-4259-7

Typeset by Intype Libra Ltd
Printed and bound in Great Britain by Page Bros, Norfolk

Contents

Contents

Preface to the Second Edition

In the six years since *Clashing Symbols* first appeared, there have been significant developments in the field of faith and culture. Therefore, when the publishers asked me to think of preparing a new version instead of doing a reprint with minor changes, I welcomed the opportunity to update the argument of these pages. Without wishing to echo advertisements for toothpaste or coffee, there is now about 20 per cent more material. The structure of the book remains the same, with the same number of chapters, but I have tried to improve and sharpen the content of each section.

What are some of the main additions? There is a new section on the French writer, René Girard, who is increasingly recognised as one of the most challenging thinkers in the field of religion and culture. Other authors, not mentioned in the first edition, and who receive some attention here include: Rowan Williams, Stanley Hauerwas, Ann Swidler, Bernard Ostry, Douglas Porpora, Jacques Godbout, Peter Berger, Mario de França Miranda, Pierangelo Sequeri and Anton Houtepen. There is more detailed space than before given to Bernard Lonergan, Charles Taylor and Karol Wojtyla (I had not studied the Pope's earlier lectures when writing in 1997). On this occasion I have also included more illustrations from imaginative literature, ranging from George Eliot to Tolkien and Douglas Coupland. The publication in 1998 of the proceedings of the Salvador Conference of World Council of Churches allowed me to bring Chapter 5 more up to date.

Four themes have undergone extensive re-writing. Inculturation: after two months teaching in Kenya in 2000 I was much more aware of tensions and conflicts in this field. Spirituality: it needed more comment on the contrast between humanistic and Christian forms of spiritual searching. Discernment: these pages were expanded in the light of several workshops I have given in these years. Postmodernity: there is now a vast literature on the religious relevance of this cultural sensibility and I wanted to do some justice to this debate.

Since working on the first edition of this book I have become a full-time teacher of fundamental theology at the Gregorian University in Rome. This academic discipline studies the credibility of faith, and can be compared to two ministries (as in a government), dealing with internal and external affairs. Its key function is to reflect on Christian revelation from within the community of believers. But it is also called to dialogue with culture in all its senses, ranging from philosophy to the lived sensibility of an epoch or people. Although this book is not a technical work of fundamental theology in the first sense, it explores the many ways in which faith interacts with its cultural contexts. Credibility of faith has many fronts: it is not just an intellectual affair. We are asked to listen to the significant movements in our world, not only in the minds of thinkers, but also in the collective imagination of ordinary people. Without such discerning attention we can neither understand our situation wisely nor fruitfully communicate Christian faith for today. This book is therefore a non-specialist contribution to fundamental theology in its task of learning from our surrounding cultures in order to make more worthy sense of faith in this moment of history.

Apart from the changes already mentioned, the introduction has also been altered considerably to evoke our fearful new world of globalisation and terrorism, and our many insecure reactions. Indeed, if I were to single out one major shift in attitude in these years it is this: we now see culture as both more central and more potentially dangerous than we realised, which seems a good reason for bringing out this new edition. It is intended to offer readers scaffolding for reflection and hope in this crucial field.

Rome
June 2003

Preface to the Second Edition

In the six years since *Clashing Symbols* first appeared, there have been significant developments in the field of faith and culture. Therefore, when the publishers asked me to think of preparing a new version instead of doing a reprint with minor changes, I welcomed the opportunity to update the argument of these pages. Without wishing to echo advertisements for toothpaste or coffee, there is now about 20 per cent more material. The structure of the book remains the same, with the same number of chapters, but I have tried to improve and sharpen the content of each section.

What are some of the main additions? There is a new section on the French writer, René Girard, who is increasingly recognised as one of the most challenging thinkers in the field of religion and culture. Other authors, not mentioned in the first edition, and who receive some attention here include: Rowan Williams, Stanley Hauerwas, Ann Swidler, Bernard Ostry, Douglas Porpora, Jacques Godbout, Peter Berger, Mario de França Miranda, Pierangelo Sequeri and Anton Houtepen. There is more detailed space than before given to Bernard Lonergan, Charles Taylor and Karol Wojtyla (I had not studied the Pope's earlier lectures when writing in 1997). On this occasion I have also included more illustrations from imaginative literature, ranging from George Eliot to Tolkien and Douglas Coupland. The publication in 1998 of the proceedings of the Salvador Conference of World Council of Churches allowed me to bring Chapter 5 more up to date.

Four themes have undergone extensive re-writing. Inculturation: after two months teaching in Kenya in 2000 I was much more aware of tensions and conflicts in this field. Spirituality: it needed more comment on the contrast between humanistic and Christian forms of spiritual searching. Discernment: these pages were expanded in the light of several workshops I have given in these years. Postmodernity: there is now a vast literature on the religious relevance of this cultural sensibility and I wanted to do some justice to this debate.

Since working on the first edition of this book I have become a full-time teacher of fundamental theology at the Gregorian University in Rome. This academic discipline studies the credibility of faith, and can be compared to two ministries (as in a government), dealing with internal and external affairs. Its key function is to reflect on Christian revelation from within the community of believers. But it is also called to dialogue with culture in all its senses, ranging from philosophy to the lived sensibility of an epoch or people. Although this book is not a technical work of fundamental theology in the first sense, it explores the many ways in which faith interacts with its cultural contexts. Credibility of faith has many fronts: it is not just an intellectual affair. We are asked to listen to the significant movements in our world, not only in the minds of thinkers, but also in the collective imagination of ordinary people. Without such discerning attention we can neither understand our situation wisely nor fruitfully communicate Christian faith for today. This book is therefore a non-specialist contribution to fundamental theology in its task of learning from our surrounding cultures in order to make more worthy sense of faith in this moment of history.

Apart from the changes already mentioned, the introduction has also been altered considerably to evoke our fearful new world of globalisation and terrorism, and our many insecure reactions. Indeed, if I were to single out one major shift in attitude in these years it is this: we now see culture as both more central and more potentially dangerous than we realised, which seems a good reason for bringing out this new edition. It is intended to offer readers scaffolding for reflection and hope in this crucial field.

Rome
June 2003

Introduction

Culture as Cinderella

> *The baffling problem of 'culture' underlies the problems of the relation of every part of the world to every other.* (T. S. Eliot)[1]

> *Everything is conditional and relational . . . This sense of things has helped to create many great civilizations and cultures.*
>
> (William Lynch)[2]

When the first edition of this book appeared in 1997, we were able to talk confidently about a century then in its closing stages. According to one version the twentieth century really began in 1917 and ended unexpectedly in 1989. Even if that remark did not apply equally to our whole planet, its point was clear: for some seventy years huge amounts of economic and political energy had been channelled into a confrontation between two ideological blocs – the capitalist and the communist. Now a few years later other battlegrounds of clashing symbols have emerged. In the midst of the euphoria surrounding the millennium, who could have fore-seen 11 September 2001? Indeed, even now, who can see its long-term impact on our sense of ourselves? Will it deepen our distrust and widen the gaps between cultural blocs in our world? Or could it paradoxically lead to new and urgent understanding across our cultural diversity? One thing is clear: what is called 'culture' has moved to centre stage in our worries and our hopes.

If we look back to the twentieth century, perhaps the gradually emerging role of culture can be recounted through a fairy story. As long as the old ideological confrontations divided the world, 'culture' was like a Cinderella waiting in the kitchen: her value was recognised by some but her public impact was small. 'Cultura' was kept in a subordinate position by the Ugly Sisters of Marxism and Atheism. These polemical sisters produced so much noise that the more subtle voice of Cultura remained unheard –

until the arrival of the Fairy Godmother, Freedom, and the invitation by Prince History to the Ball celebrating the end of Modernity. Without forcing the details too much, this version of the Cinderella story suggests that cultural insights were neglected in the era of dualist oppositions, and that as we leave behind the false clarities of 'modernity', we come to appreciate culture as an essential way of interpreting the hatreds that divide our planet as well as new hopes for a more-than-economic globalisation. September 11, in this light, was a terrible confirmation that we had entered the complexity of postmodernity. The tools of advanced technology were used to destroy symbols of power. But, on reflection, that tragic event was the death certificate of old clarities. On that day black-and-white contrasts of cultural blocs gave way to enforced diversity. Of course there remains the temptation to respond to the new within the framework of the old, simply to proclaim a 'war against terrorism' as if the battle lines were still black and white. The first question from God to human beings in the Bible is 'Where are you?' The first question of Jesus in the gospel of John is 'What are you looking for?' Together these two questions are in tune with the mood of these years of after-shock. Where are we and what do we really want? To ponder those questions means asking how culture shapes our self-images and how we shape culture. In that sense the content of these pages has its minor contribution to make to finding our way more wisely in this fragile time.

Falling walls and towers

The fall of the Berlin Wall was the event that best symbolised the end of one cultural epoch and the fall of the twin towers symbolised the inauguration of another. Many people may remember a strange scene that was shown on television screens during that celebrated year of 1989: the rather gentle lowering to the ground of statues of Lenin or Marx in various countries of the communist bloc. And the empty pedestals raised various questions: what will take their place? will more invisible idols come to power? Did we get our unexpected and frightening answer with what is called 9/11?

If 1989 began the public funeral of modernity, events since then confirm the coming of age of so-called postmodernity – a cultural phase that claims various birthdays, ranging from as early as Nietzsche's philosophy to the social and political upheavals of the year 1968. During modernity we had expressed our commitments according to one or other ideological stance. The events of 9/11 may come to symbolise our postmodern fate, our entering into a phase of unknowing, no longer sure of how to define ourselves. More dangerously we see our potential for prejudice and for wars, whether of propaganda or blood, between the world's major cultural blocs – most obviously between Islam and the so-called Christian West.

With the demise of walls and the crumbling of towers, not only has culture emerged from the shadows in a positive sense: its darker potentials are also making themselves felt. We are all cultural animals, both in its humanising and dehumanising meanings. In a now famous and controversial article, entitled 'The Clash of Civilizations?', Professor Samuel Huntington of Harvard University argued that future conflicts 'will not be primarily ideological or primarily economic. The great divisions among humankind and the dominating source of conflict will be cultural,' and he added that cultural characteristics change less easily than political and economic ones. Thus our new sense of plurality reveals a darker and more conflictual dimension. It is another angle to the Cinderella insight: 'the Velvet Curtain of culture has replaced the Iron Curtain of ideology as the most significant dividing line'.[3] The second Gulf War and other tensions between 'Western civilisation' and the Islamic world would seem to support this thesis.

Cultural horizons of globalisation

If these years have witnessed many dents in our armour of naive optimism, it has also seen an explosion of debate and concern about what is called globalisation. Nobody denies the existence of this phenomenon, with its roots in the fields of technology and economics, but there are widely different interpretations of its nature and even more so of its cultural impact. Clearly we have entered a new global phase of history, where increasingly 'we all make up one world, even if we are only gradually coming to recognise it'.[4] The potentially positive side is that in the 'global village', where one can see events within minutes on the television screen, a consensus can emerge that is more aware of injustices. The negative side is that this image world is in danger of becoming an anti-culture of commercial triviality, and hence a highly questionable form of uniformity. Many voices warn us that we are moving towards 'a memory-less culture' without identity and without history.[5] Others tell us that globalisation is a 'complex and brutal' system, and that there is really nobody in control.[6] Pope John Paul's statements on globalisation see it as an ambiguous phenomenon – as a source both of promise and of concern. Speaking to the Academy of Social Sciences (27.4.01), he identified some key issues in these words, underlining the link between globalisation as an economic development and its more hidden cultural impact:

> Globalization, a priori, is neither good nor bad. It will be what people make of it ... One of the Church's concerns about globalization is that it has quickly become a cultural phenomenon. The market as an exchange mechanism has become the medium of a new culture ...
>
> What is happening is that changes in technology and work relationships are moving too quickly for cultures to respond ...
>
> Ethical discernment in the context of globalization must be based upon two inseparable principles ... The human being must always be an end and not a means ... Second, no external power has the right to downplay and still less to destroy the value of human cultures.
>
> Globalization must not be a new version of colonialism. It must respect the diversity of cultures, which, within the universal harmony of peoples, are life's interpretative keys.

The debate around globalisation and culture needs the challenge of that principled vision, but of course many unresolved questions remain. In the words of Konrad Raiser, General Secretary of the World Council of Churches, can we hope for a 'global community whose interdependence is not reduced to trade'?[7] Is globalisation producing a specific and new culture worldwide? Or could it be a force for responsible human interaction on a scale never before possible in history and respectful of diversity of culture? Is it a process where nobody is in command and, if so, is it wishful thinking to advocate ethical or moral controls for globalisation? Who is to be believed, the optimists who interpret it as gradually extending new benefits to all parts of the world, or the pessimists who see it as a new colonialism where the powerful expand their dominance? Is it mainly a market-driven force that puts local cultures in danger of losing their identities?

On that last point there is some evidence of surprising strength within cultures. Remembering the suggestion that 'culture' is less immediately visible than 'society', perhaps consumerism is more social than cultural in its influence. Some cultural groupings remain remarkably resistant to the levelling tendencies of the global village. In cultures as diverse as those of Africa or Japan, the repercussions of global lifestyles seem marginal in comparison with the differentness that remains. More politically, there are tendencies within Islam or Hinduism, where religious cultures have become militantly assertive over self-identity. Thus the impact of the media-culture of 'mascara and soap opera' (a phrase from Julia Kristeva) can be shallow in two senses: on the surface and silly. Where people are without strong anchors of belonging, television trash can easily have a dehumanising and culturally destructive impact. But any theory about the trivialising impact of the media has to take account of a contrary reality – the survival of deep cultural differences between peoples. Culture now means 'cultures', to echo the Mexican writer Octavio Paz, and they have surprising survival strengths.

Many other related questions arise in our brave new world, full of fears as well as full of exciting newness. Instead of fostering a more integrated world could globalisation be a force of marginalisation and segregation? Are we creating a 'digital divide', in the sense of a developed world galloping into undreamed-of sophistication of technology and whole continents and peoples where these tools seem like science fiction? What will be the long-term impact of migration? Already the United States has more Hispanics than

Afro-Americans and Western Europe has increasing minorities of
Muslims.

Since the first edition of this book a new word has been coined
to indicate a whole new generation of the young and not so young:
they are 'netigens' rather than citizens. Their world is increasingly
the excitingly navigable cyberspace called Internet (with 'chat'
and other attractions healthy and unhealthy). No doubt future
historians of culture will see this face of globalisation as a potential
shift in our sense of knowledge and reality. Experts such as Derrick
de Kerckhove (director of the McLuhan Project in Canada) are
telling us that the electronic information revolution puts us excitingly in a new moment of evolution and yet he acknowledges its
profound ambiguity. Will it imprison people in a selfish privacy?
Or will it prove an extraordinary source of interactive spirituality?
Already the Irish Jesuit website called Sacred Space, which offers
daily direction in prayer, is a huge success affecting thousands of
'users' mainly on weekdays. But of course pornography remains
the biggest moneymaker on the web, and much 'adult' material is
available even to children without paying.

Cultural studies and religion

It is not only in the field of global analysis that 'culture' has
emerged as a key concept in recent years. A relatively new discipline called cultural studies has arrived in many universities and
its tendency here is to study culture as 'a moral activity' and to
focus on the 'making of meaning' in contemporary society; it also
tries to examine the interaction between power, values, mass media
and imagination.[8] There is a widespread insistence that 'cultural
studies' represents a radical break with the old stratifications
between 'high' and 'low' culture and that it aims at more than a
description of ways of life: it wants to investigate how the production and consumption of cultural images is controlled in
different societies. In any bookshop with academic pretensions,
one will find a section devoted to 'cultural studies': largely under
the influence of postmodernism (a subject in a later chapter here)
these authors seek often to unmask the falsities of our assumptions

in such areas as politics, gender, race relations, education, mass media and religion.

This book will take a largely religious perspective on cultural analysis and hence there is no need to dwell on this aspect here. However, one can mention that culture, as a hidden censor of what is socially acceptable, was a key concern in Stephen Carter's bestseller *The Culture of Disbelief*. Since North American culture is rapidly becoming a presence in lived culture around the globe, Carter's argument is relevant beyond the borders of the United States or his particular specialisation in constitutional law. In brief, he diagnoses how the pressures of contemporary culture keep religion impotent in the public sphere. The message is that 'it is perfectly all right to *believe* that stuff' provided you keep it to yourself; in other words, the only form of religion permitted becomes a 'trivialization of faith', something on the level of a hobby, but 'not really a fit activity for intelligent, public-spirited adults'.[9]

This kind of 'secular marginalisation' (as it will be called in the chapter on cultural discernment) has also been a focus for theological reflection, because the very possibility of religious faith today is influenced by cultural factors. Our receptivity for revelation is more shaped by culture than by philosophical clarities. We seldom live by ideas or ideologies but rather by images of life communicated by our surrounding worlds. Hence the cultural wavelength is central for understanding the shifting currents within religious commitment now. As will be argued later, various forms of 'cultural unbelief' now constitute the main family of distance from faith or rejection of religion.

In the complex and pluralist world on the move, it is an urgent task for theology to understand why the Christian vision, which had such eloquent and encompassing impact on people in the past, seems to have lost meaningfulness in today's cultural situation. The insight that cultural change influences the agenda of theology was symbolised in the opening sentence of Bernard Lonergan's *Method in Theology*, with its claim that 'theology mediates between a cultural matrix and the significance and role of religion in that matrix'. And he goes on at once to note that once the meaning of culture widens from the 'classical notion' to the 'empirical notion of culture' as involving ways of life, then theology is no longer a matter of ageless or 'permanent achievement' but is recognised as 'an ongoing process'.[10] In his judgement the contemporary world is undergoing 'a crisis not of faith but of culture'.[11]

In addition there is a new centrality of culture within church discourse, as different key words have come to prominence in Catholicism in these recent decades. Thus, 'dialogue' and then 'justice' were the new words of the sixties and seventies, followed by 'new evangelisation' and 'culture' during the eighties and nineties. At the same time the relations between faith and culture have become the object of intense debate – especially with regard to 'inculturation'. Religion and culture have had a reciprocal relationship in every epoch of history until the recent centuries in the West. That the Western Christian Churches represent a small minority of Christian believers in the world has been known for decades. Now this inevitable demographic shift from the richer world is being seen as a cultural phenomenon that will gradually change our sense of religious identity. Within all the Christian Churches it is in non-Western countries that the most lively languages of faith are being born.

Complex and omnipresent

The phenomenon called culture is an exclusively human experience, as a simple example can show. Unlike many animals, a newborn infant has little genetic programming to guide its behaviour; instead of being able to survive on its own, the human baby needs others for a considerable time before arriving at independence. Culture is the human learning space where the child develops its open-ended potentials for growth. And, unlike the animals, this adventure of cultural learning is 'not simply about behaviour. It is also about ideas,' involving patterns of meaning, embodied in symbols, and subject to considerable evolution and even conscious change.[12] From birth we are all surrounded by this omnipresent and seemingly omnipotent complex called culture, which is both external and internal, both observable and concealed.

The more one thinks about it, the field of culture seems full of contradictory tendencies. It does not point clearly and constantly in one direction. Instead it sends out contrary signals. Thus we speak in the one breath of the relativising of Western culture and about the global village created by Western-style communications and technology. We talk about the rise of secular culture, but we are witnessing a surprising turn-around in this area. Thirty or so years ago many sociologists argued confidently about an 'irreversible secularization', predicting that religion would inevitably decline in influence and become something socially marginal. More recently we have heard about the 'return of religion', the rise of fundamentalism, the claims of faith within the public sphere, the multiplying of new religious movements, and the many-faceted spiritual exploration called 'New Age'. Strangely, both the floating religiousness and the fundamentalist rigidity may have the same origin – a desire to escape complexity and find anchors. These seemingly contrary phenomena are provoked by the fragmentations, the malnutritions and the rootless loneliness of a dominantly secular culture.

An unrecognised ocean

What is culture for our purposes in this book? The term is used here mainly in its broad anthropological meaning – as a cluster of assumptions, values and ways of life – rather than in its older and more elite meaning connected with intellectual or artistic activity. The next chapter will explore some of the many meanings associated with culture. Monsieur Jourdain, in Molière's *Le Bourgeois Gentilhomme*, made the much-mocked discovery that he had been speaking prose all his life and had not known it. What is comic is that his teacher had given him only a word and not an insight. We are all living within a culture but to grasp its significance involves a series of surprises and awakenings. One can clarify, as is often done, the enlargement of the term 'culture' from the sphere of thought or artistic expression or conscious human development, to the more inclusive sense of culture as indicating lifestyles and assumptions. Though important as a starting point, this descriptive approach misses the power of culture as involving not simply a neutral cluster of behaviour patterns or values, but a hidden set of control mechanisms that shape our sensibility and our 'structure of feeling'.[13] Culture can be an unrecognised presence, 'a highly selective screen' between us and our world which decides 'what we pay attention to and what we ignore'.[14] Thus culture is quite simply the main influence on how we see ourselves (what contemporary theorists call our 'social imaginary'), and it is all the more potent for being largely concealed in its impact.

Later in these pages various interpretations and definitions of culture will be explored but for the moment I would like to quote an attractive and eloquent account of culture offered a quarter of a century ago by Bernard Ostry:[15]

> Culture, however we define it, is central to everything we
>   do and think.
> It is what we do and the reason why we do it,
> what we wish and why we imagine it,
> what we perceive and how we express it,
> how we live and in what manner we approach death.
> It is our environment and the patterns of our adaptation to it.
> It is the world we have created and are still creating;
> it is the way we see that world and the motives that urge us
>   to change it.
> It is the way we know ourselves and each other;
> it is our web of personal relationships,
> it is the images and abstractions that allow us to live together
>   in communities and nations.
> It is the element in which we live.

In somewhat more aggressive tone Immanuel Wallerstein has described culture as a trap 'overlain by much protective shrubbery which hides its outline and ferocity from us'.[16] In this light, perhaps a series of metaphoric parallels can begin to evoke the inescapable role culture plays in shaping our sense of identity, because it forms our mind-sets and heart-sets and gives us our typical way of interpreting our lives.

Culture therefore is like:

• an ocean, surrounding us as water a fish;

• an environment that seems natural, especially if it is the only one we know;

- a lens, something we see through without realising that it is not the only way of seeing;
- a transmitter sending subliminal messages, that affect our priorities without us knowing;
- a filter, allowing through certain images of normality but not others;
- a set of codes, like writing, which is artificial but comes to be second nature;
- a complex traffic light that signals what one should pay attention to;
- the air we breathe, that may be healthy or polluted;
- a language not just of words, but of expectations we learn to obey;
- a set of blinkers, censoring what can be seen;
- a cage that is there and not there, like a mime artist pretending to be inside a glass box;
- an iceberg of the common sense of a group, which stays submerged or unconscious;
- a baby's building bricks, the basis for creating a world;
- a flight recorder preserving the memory of humanity's journey;
- a life agenda that controls the conversation about existence;
- a womb, within which one feels perfectly at home, not knowing there are other worlds;
- an accumulation of unacknowledged habits, like an addiction that resists recognition;
- a conspiracy of silence, imposed by the past;
- a menu of existence, either 'fixed' or à la carte': either way the choices have limits;
- a playground of possibilities, inviting one to creative freedom;
- an ever-present horizon, beyond which one cannot see.

In this random litany of images there are tensions between evocations of being trapped and those that suggest space for movement. Both can be true of 'lived' culture: it can encourage creativity or it can prove imprisoning. What all these metaphors have in common is the implication that culture is usually a hidden persuader in our lives. It involves a convergence of massaging messages (as Marshall McLuhan might say) that lull us into assuming that all this is natural. Whereas the root meaning of culture – from *colere* in Latin, to till or cultivate – suggests that it is the opposite of natural. In fact it is whatever we have made, whether a Tower of Babel or a Sistine Chapel. It is a human invention over a long time. Although nothing about culture is necessary or inevitable, when we swim in this ocean or see through this lens or receive the transmissions of this force around us, everything seems utterly normal and neutral. Awakening to its nonneutrality is a first step towards a Christian response to culture in practice.

Against the background of lively cultural debates in many fields, this book has a fairly modest scope: to present aspects of the faith –culture relationship as it has evolved within recent decades. The aim is to introduce the reader to the principal insights and controversies being discussed by both individual thinkers and church bodies concerned with this theme. Early chapters explore the range of meaning of 'culture'. Next some sections focus on church developments in understanding and responding to culture. Themes concerning modernity and postmodernity are then given fairly extended treatment, especially from a religious point of view. The final four chapters deal with more 'pastoral' issues – inculturation, discernment, youth ministry and the outlines of a spirituality for today's culture.

'At the heart of every culture lies the attitude a person takes to the greatest mystery, the mystery of God.' Thus wrote Pope John Paul II in *Centesimus annus* (No. 24). The aim of this book is to provide a theology of nonpanic and of liberation for believers faced with their changing cultures. Nonpanic means reading the situation with wisdom but without complacency. We are all aware now of how a polluted environment can cause serious illness. There is a more subtle field of spiritual health, where invasive cultural influences can kidnap our imagination.

This book proposes a Christian ecology of the imagination. Insofar as we are free *from* the potentially negative forces in our cultures, we will be truly free *for* faith, and for a creative Christian life that does not just discern culture but hopes to transform it in the light of the gospel.

Chapter One

Clarifying the Concept

Culture is not only what we live by. It is also, in great measure, what we live for. (Terry Eagleton)[1]

Culture is a way of life and how this way of life is experienced, understood, and interpreted. Both theology and culture are ambiguous and dynamic – capable of oppressing and of liberating.

(Marilyn Legge)[2]

In the nineteenth century two famous accounts of culture appeared within two years of each other, and between them they point to two main schools of interpretation of this concept. In 1869 Matthew Arnold published *Culture and Anarchy* where he argued that culture meant 'the pursuit of perfection' which entailed 'an inward condition of the mind and spirit', a quality 'at variance with the mechanical and material civilisation' of that industrial age. In his view culture meant the 'pursuit of sweetness and light' through becoming acquainted with the best that has been thought and said in world history.[3]

By contrast, in 1871, the British anthropologist Edward Tylor published his pioneering work entitled *Primitive Culture*, where he offered one of the earliest of non-Arnoldian definitions of culture: 'Culture or civilization is that complex whole which includes knowledge, belief, art, morals, law, custom, and any other capabilities and habits acquired by man as a member of society.'[4]

Culture remains one of those words that can be exasperating in its inclusiveness. It can seem to be a chameleon term that changes its significance depending on the user. But in fact most of its meanings offer variations on either the Arnold or the Tylor tradition. When Arnold wrote in that eloquent style, he could be fairly confident that 'cultured' people would understand him – even if those he called 'barbarians' might not. His elite audience shared with him a sense that culture pointed to the highest available expressions of human vision and human value. But to say that is to beg the question: who decides what is best? Obviously, the 'cultured'! Thus behind the Arnoldian theory lay a strangely circular field of argument: 'cultural' leaders had a monopoly on what 'culture' means. They exalted the 'classics' as models to be imitated. The very notion of having classic works of art implied permanent values, a core of stable excellence amid the changes of history. In short this view of culture was traditional and normative, and it had prevailed in Western education for centuries. A contemporary philosopher has voiced his general agreement with Arnold's view of culture in these words: 'The high culture of our civilisation contains knowledge which is far more significant than anything that can be absorbed from the channels of popular communication.'[5]

In spite of Arnold, until fairly recently the word 'culture' was less widely used in English than in Latin languages. The French novelist André Malraux, who was Minister for Culture under General de Gaulle, said that culture is what answers our human questions about what we are doing here in this world. Every day a national radio news in Italy ends with 'la pagina culturale' – the cultural page, meaning some event in the world of art or music or books. However, the *Sunday Times* publishes a fat weekly supplement called 'Culture', where it is largely the Arnoldian meaning that is intended. These pages deal with theatre, art, books, music, cinema and so on. Arnold might well be shocked at some of the contents of the films or the admission of 'pop' music into this section, but he would at least recognise the field. Thus in everyday usage 'culture' retains its creative or aesthetic meaning, even if the term has enlarged its territory of significance in ways that Arnold did not foresee and might not approve.

Especially during the first half of the twentieth century anthropologists and sociologists developed Tylor's approach and gave 'culture' a much wider meaning, so that it became almost synonymous with a way of life, and less associated with the worlds of thought or art. People speak not only of a 'culture of self-development' (which at least echoes the Latin origin of growth) but even of a 'culture of violence'. In a recent radio interview I heard criticism of a 'political culture of bribery'. Clearly this second set of meanings would not fit into that Sunday cultural supplement: it points instead to a cluster of assumptions about what is acceptable within a certain context. As the late Archbishop Worlock once put it, with Liverpool-style bluntness, culture is simply 'the way we do things around here'.[6] Whatever is the 'done thing' can still dominate within more cohesive cultures, but as soon as people move away from the confines of home or traditional settings, they discover that there is more than one way of doing things: at this point an awareness of cultural diversity makes everything seem more complex and can dramatically change the agenda of religious adherence and religious belonging. In Kathryn's Tanner's words, 'though culture is universal in the sense that all people have one, the anthropological use of the term highlights human diversity' and the attributes of a particular group of people.[7]

One recalls the famous remark of Goering that when he heard the word culture he wanted to reach for his gun. He probably had the more elite meaning in mind – the world of art or ideas. If he experienced today's extension of 'culture' and the diversification of 'cultures', he might well reach for a heavier weapon. And yet the word seems here to stay. Whatever about niceties of vocabulary or emphasis, it is now a part of our general 'culture' to realise that 'culture' constitutes a total context that shapes us all, and this stress on the hidden power of culture goes beyond the more descriptive stance of both Arnold and Tylor. The Arnold emphasis dealt with what can be called 'objective' or 'conscious' culture, highlighting such cultural products as art and institutions. The Tylor approach focused more on 'subjective' or 'invisible' culture, including all the modes of meaning and perception that people assimilate within a society.

Later in these pages we shall see that the supremacy of these two schools of thinking about culture has been challenged in recent decades by more explanatory, penetrating and socio-political questions. Do we construct culture or does culture construct us? What is the process of production behind the accepted forms and practices of culture? Who controls the vehicles of cultural formation? How can we participate in the creation of culture? As will be seen when Raymond Williams and René Girard are discussed in the next chapter, culture may be not simply a humanising force (à la Arnold) or a merely neutral field of unity of lifestyles (à la Tylor): it can be a violent minefield of conflicting urges and images. Even though culture offers us tools and rituals to cope with the world's strangeness, it also provides us with sources of antagonism, power games and mutual prejudice. Instead of being a source of social cohesion and coherence, contemporary views of culture insist that it has 'shattered into diverse domains where rival elements stand alongside each other, without the possibility of overview or synthesis'[8]. But for the moment we concentrate on mainstream approaches to the description of culture.

Six categories

Initial help in this task can be had from a now famous book of 1952, which listed some 164 definitions of culture, categorising them into six major groups and further sub-groups.[9] That exercise in clarification remains extremely useful but it needs adaptation to include the many new emphases of the last fifty years. I propose here to summarise that classic work of Kroeber and Kluckhohn, to review some key contributions of more recent decades, and then to outline an updated model for understanding the diversity of meaning of 'culture' today, keeping in mind the scope of these pages – the relation of culture to faith and of faith to culture.

Six principal categories of definitions of culture were identified by Kroeber and Kluckhohn.

1.   The first kind consists of *descriptive* accounts of culture, which seek to list the key elements that make up the *'complex whole'* that is culture. Indeed that phrase, as already seen, was first used by Edward Tylor in 1871 and was repeated in their respective definitions of culture by Ruth Benedict in 1929 and by Margaret Mead in 1937. Hence the first key to understanding culture is its non-simplicity: it refers to a coming together of different elements such as meanings, values, symbols, beliefs, practices and so on. Some thinkers will question the emphasis on unity or a 'whole', insisting that culture study is often tempted to find patterns of coherence at the expense of the inevitable pluralism within a culture; but

practically nobody disagrees as to the converging complex that is culture.

2. A second ingredient in definitions of culture is some *historical dimension*, in the sense that culture is received as a 'social heritage' from the past, and thus is communicated from one generation to another.

3. Third, a culture is viewed as involving a particular set of assumptions about values and behaviour, and hence it contains certain *normative elements* that influence the life of a group. Some experts here introduce a distinction between 'culture' as referring to the way of life of all groups, and 'a culture' as pointing to the specific modes of behaviour that are accepted in a given society.

4. Fourth, some definitions deal with the *psychological functions* served by culture, for instance in creating security through traditional responses to such great human issues as sexuality or death, or as answering the need for social order through systems of law or organisation. Thus culture has a formative role where people learn how to cope with life in ways that have been tested in the past. It provides a *philosophy* or a *cosmology* to answer some of the fundamental questions about life.

5. Fifth, culture provides a *structure* for living together, both a structure of meaning and an inherited way of organising relations between people. Some cultures will be more rooted in authority and others favour looser forms of cohesion and belonging, but some structuring of social life is a constant across different forms of culture.

6. Sixth, some approaches tackle the question of the *genesis* of culture, and these tend to stress that culture is not simply an automatic inheritance between generations but a conscious human product, born of different forms of human association. In the words of Clyde Kluckhohn, 'culture designates those aspects of the total human environment, tangible and intangible, that have been created' by human beings themselves.[10] In so far as culture is therefore a human product, some authors highlight the fact that humans are symbol-using animals and hence that symbols rather

than concepts are the natural vehicles for mediating the meanings and values embodied in cultures.

Before trying to offer a somewhat different synthesis of essential elements for an understanding of culture – one that can serve the more specifically religious purposes of this book – it may be useful to see how these six elements are either present or absent in a few more recent accounts of culture. From a vast field I single out three English-language approaches because of their diversity from one another, and also because they highlight aspects partially neglected in the summary of Kroeber and Kluckhohn.

Geertz, Lonergan, Williams

According to a widely quoted definition offered by Clifford Geertz, culture 'denotes an historically transmitted pattern of meanings embodied in symbols, a system of inherited conceptions expressed in symbolic forms by means of which men communicate, perpetuate, and develop their knowledge about and attitudes toward life'.[11] In his own words, he espouses a 'semiotic' concept of culture, in the sense that he seeks to study the sign systems underlying human behaviour. He compares culture to 'webs of significance' that humanity has spun, and any analysis of culture will try to understand the complex meaning embodied in those social and symbolic webs.[12] By coincidence, the Latin for 'web' is *textum*, and some more recent thinkers like to speak about 'culture texts': 'a text can be a set of words, an event, or even a person. Culture then becomes the total sum of these texts shared by a given people.'[13]

Geertz, unlike most of the authors cited by Kroeber and Kluckhohn, gives prominence to the crucial role of symbols as carriers of culture, and this aspect seems of special relevance in reflecting on the relations of culture and religious faith. By placing symbolic communication at the core of his definition, he situates culture in the public realm rather than in some personal inner self. He is also seeking to do justice to the 'informal logic of actual life', holding that 'society's forms are culture's substance'.[14] Apart from this new priority to symbols, in fact his definition touches on four of the six key elements mentioned above: historical transmission (no. 2), more philosophical-psychological dimensions (no. 4), culture as a context that provides 'control mechanisms'[15] (no. 5) and which embodies itself in symbolic forms (no. 6). Interestingly, in this short definition, Geertz does not suggest anything about the 'complex whole' that culture entails; at one point he speaks of an 'accumulated totality',[16] but generally he is more aware of the diversity of culture than of its unity. He has moved away from the older 'functionalist' approach, which highlighted how elements in a culture interrelate and have different purposes in creating social cohesion. The functionalist school had tended to neglect the symbolic wavelength of culture, but in fact cultural models serve both as 'social artifacts and as cognitive representations'.[17]

In a later book Geertz broadens the agenda to include 'common sense' as 'an everywhere-found cultural form' of a less tightly integrated kind, expressed in the 'of-courseness' of different cultures.[18] This links up with the emphasis on hidden assumptions that was discussed in the introductory chapter here. Lived culture is practically identical with the common sense of a society, and as such can be a major obstacle or ally for religious faith. Geertz sums up the omnipresence of this cultural system in an eloquent passage:

> Religion rests its case on revelation, science on method, ideology on moral passion; but common sense rests its on the assertion that it is not a case at all, just life in a nutshell. The world is its authority.[19]

Ann Swidler has usefully united these two aspects of culture – the symbolic and the everyday – in her description, stressing that culture offers people a range of tools to choose from in order to construct strategies of action.

> Culture consists of such symbolic vehicles of meaning, including beliefs, ritual practices, art forms, and ceremonies, as well as informal cultural practices such as language, gossip, stories, and rituals of daily life.[20]

The Canadian thinker Bernard Lonergan, who was mentioned briefly in the Introduction, came to highlight the crucial importance of culture for theology. Indeed, as already mentioned, the opening sentence of his book *Method in Theology* announces a surprising emphasis: the task of theology is to mediate between a cultural context and the role of religion in that context. In his earlier period he had seen culture in its 'high' sense as the human capacity to explore and inquire:

> Man can pause and with a smile or a forced grin ask what the drama, what he himself is about. His culture is his capacity to ask, to reflect, to reach an answer that at once satisfies his intelligence and speaks to his heart.[21]

In a later phase he spoke of the transition from one dominant view of culture to another as constituting a major crisis of meaning in today's world. The old understanding of culture was 'classicist' and presumed a stable and unchanging world order: culture was always in the singular and implied the established meanings and values of Western civilisation. The classicist mentality tended to ignore the movement of history and to think that its formulations of truth were permanent summits of wisdom. Hence the classicist mentality did not really take cultural diversity seriously. Immutability was the criterion of value. Any changes that might happen were secondary and relegated to the category of unimportant 'accidentals'. But this proud set of securities has broken down and its collapse has caused deep confusion, not least inside the Catholic Church. Its place has been taken by an 'empirical' view of culture, influenced by a whole series of developments in recent centuries: the new methods in science (empiricism), the recognition of different worldviews (pluralism), the rise of the human sciences (especially anthropology and sociology), the realisation that history and culture are human products, always ambiguous and relative. In Lonergan's own summary:

> The contemporary notion of culture is empirical. A culture is a set of meanings and values informing a common way of life, and there are as many cultures as there are distinct sets of such meanings and values. However, this manner of conceiving culture is relatively recent. It is the product of empirical human studies. Within less than one hundred years it has replaced an older, classicist view that had flourished for over

two millennia. On the older view culture was conceived not empirically but normatively. It was the opposite of barbarism . . . It stressed not facts but values. It could not but claim to be universalist.[22]

With the term 'informing', used in the sense of giving form to (rather than modern 'information'), Lonergan bridges the inner world of philosophies and the outer world of shared patterns of life. For him, however, it is not precise enough to identify culture with what (as we will see) Raymond Williams calls a 'whole way of life'; culture underlies our ways of living, and hence is a more subtle and invisible presence than society. Moreover Lonergan stresses that culture involves a communal expression of 'inter-subjectivity' and 'meaning', where we embody our self-under-standings in many ways – in art, language and in how we live and act.[23] In this perspective culture is in constant dialogue between its two dimensions, one more invisible and one more visible. We can describe the complex patterns of a way of life – that is the level of anthropology; but we need also to inquire further into the world-views behind or beneath that external realm of shared life. There is constant interaction between the more hidden sets of assumptions (meanings and values) and the more manifest field of observable social patterns (common ways of life) and of conscious interpre-tations (philosophies etc.). In Lonergan's words, besides the meaning and value immediately intuited, felt, spoken, acted out, there is to any advanced culture a 'superstructure', where this lived vision is worked out 'in a far more reflective, deliberate, critical fashion'.[24]

With the demise of old 'classicist' assumptions, a radically dif-ferent notion of culture took over, where it 'denotes something found in every people, for in every people there is some apprehen-sion of meaning and value in their way of life. So it is that modern culture is the culture that knows about other cultures, that relates them to one another genetically, that knows all of them to be man-made.'[25] Lonergan also recognises the relevance of this transition for the communication of religious faith. Where the older school of missionary work would happily, and perhaps unconsciously, 'impose' its culture on other people, the cultural pluralist will recognise a multiplicity of cultural traditions. Therefore 'he would proceed from within their culture and he would seek ways and means for making it into a vehicle for communicating the Christian message'.[26] Before the word came into vogue Lonergan was already touching on some key elements in 'inculturation'.

The view of culture proposed by the British writer Raymond Williams has some parallels to Lonergan although they were not aware of one another's writings and Williams does not deal with religious themes. At times Williams seems remarkably close to the words of the Canadian theologian: thus in 1961 he wrote of the analysis of culture as entailing 'the clarification of the meanings and values implicit and explicit in a particular way of life'.[27] He went on to describe the culture of any given period as a 'structure of feeling', born from a process of 'interaction between patterns learned and created in the mind and patterns communicated and made active in relationships, conventions and institutions'.[28]

Apart from being Professor of Drama at Cambridge University, he had a lifelong passion for researching the changing culture of recent centuries. In his view the evolution of the idea of culture mirrors our responses to the huge changes in social conditions and in human relationships since the industrial revolution. As early as 1958 he summarised the story of the term 'culture' as follows:

> it had meant, primarily, the 'tending of natural growth', and then, by analogy, a process of human training. But this latter use, which had usually been a culture *of* something, was changed, in the nineteenth century, to *culture* as such, a thing in itself. It came to mean, first 'a general state or habit of the mind', having close relations with the ideal of human perfection. Second, it came to mean 'the general state of intel-lectual development, in a society as a whole'. Third, it came to mean 'the general body of the arts'. Fourth, later in the century, it came to mean 'a whole way of life, material, intellec-tual and spiritual'.[29]

In a more personal essay of that same year he wrote that 'Culture is ordinary: that is the first fact', in the sense that every society has its own purposes and meanings which it embodies in 'a whole way of life'.[30] In a later book he traces the shift in meaning of 'culture' from the 'active cultivation' of the mind to a 'configuration' of the spirit of a people in the eighteenth century. In the next century anthropology stressed the plural nature of culture as pointing to distinctive ways of life. Later still came a more 'materialist' sense of culture as a direct or indirect 'product' of 'cultural practice' within a given social order.[31] From this materialist point of view, shifts in sensibility are nearly always linked to changes in economic systems and work patterns which in turn influence lifestyles.

As well as being a historian Williams was a socialist who liked to stress particular cultures as products of specific social situations. At times he seems to accept the interpretation of culture as primarily a way of life: 'a culture is not only a body of intellectual and imaginative work; it is also and essentially a whole way of life'.[32] But often he wants to go beyond this descriptive approach, expressing a certain impatience with the neutrality and even innocence of definitions which do not 'make room for study of manifestly signifying institutions, practices and works'.[33] To do justice to the complex realities of modern societies it is necessary to see culture as a *product* of definite forces at work in history and to inquire how it is *embedded* in a whole range of activities. Hence Williams prefers to define culture as 'the signifying system through which... a social order is communicated, reproduced, experienced, and explored'.[34] One could say that Williams is making his own fusion of three of the six elements of Kroeber and Kluckhohn as listed earlier (the normative, structural and genetic approaches to culture), but with his more politically alert philosophy, he seeks to question the whole set of 'practices' implicit in any culture, asking in particular about 'the means of cultural production'[35] – the influences behind the particular features of a dominant culture.

It is worth adding that the French philosopher and sociologist Pierre Bourdieu echoes Raymond Williams' emphasis on 'practices' as the key to understanding culture but he gives pride of place to what he calls 'habitus': by this he means a system of ever-changing 'mental dispositions' underlying the 'values which dominate the whole of our experience'. Deeply linked with language – that central but elusive carrier of cultural attitudes – the 'habitus' is shaped through all the agents that have an impact on an individual, from parents to education to the symbolic power of institutions and social hierarchies.[36] Once again we are forced to recognise the doubleness of culture: it involves observable practices or socially legitimated ways of acting but it also entails a more concealed set of subjective attitudes often assimilated unconsciously over a long time. Together these habits of acting and of interpreting can either imprison people within prejudices or they can become avenues towards authentic living, towards self-transcending choices that challenge the negative bias of any culture.

Towards a synthesis

Faced with this diversity of approach to culture, one becomes aware of significant tensions between one emphasis and another. For the sake of simplicity, one could suggest three main schools among the several tendencies just mentioned: the *neutral* description of culture as a convergence of various elements in human society and history; the *idealist* tendency to highlight meanings, ideas, symbols and values; a more *political and moral* sense of culture as conditioning human choices and actions and therefore as having often unconscious power over human behaviour.

In the light of the multi-faceted nature of culture, one can appreciate the rich synthesis offered by the UNESCO definition, which is the product of an international conference on 'Cultural Policies', held in Mexico in 1982. This complex statement seeks to do justice both to the 'creative' or conscious culture exemplified by the imaginative, intellectual and spiritual dimensions of life, and to the more 'lived' sense of culture associated with anthropology and sociology:

> Culture may now be said to be the whole complex of distinctive spiritual, material, intellectual and emotional features that characterize a society or social group. It includes not only the arts and letters, but also modes of life, the fundamental rights of the human being, value systems, traditions and beliefs . . . It is culture that gives man the ability to reflect upon himself. It is culture that makes us specifically human, rational

beings, endowed with a critical judgment and a sense of moral commitment. It is through culture that we discern values and make choices. It is through culture that man expresses himself, becomes aware of himself, recognizes his incompleteness, questions his own achievements, seeks untiringly for new meanings and creates works through which he transcends his limitations.[37]

This remarkable gathering of insights begins by echoing the 'complex whole' expression of Edward Tylor. Of the remaining five dimensions of culture, as mentioned above, the UNESCO account is strangely silent on the historical process of communicating human vision across generations, but it includes in one way or another all the other four aspects: normative 'value systems'; psychological and philosophical quest for 'new meanings'; the 'material' structures of a 'tradition'; and this text is quite eloquent about culture as productive and active in its exploration of human experience. In this way it takes the more anthropological question about the 'genesis' of culture and enlarges it to cover the whole adventure of 'spiritual' awareness and of how a human being 'transcends' the limits of one's situation. It is worth noting that these two words ('spiritual' and 'transcends') are the first and last key words of this whole statement, thus leaving it much more open to the religious horizon than any of the more academic descriptions of culture cited earlier in this chapter.

In the light of all this, we can attempt a synthesis of the multidimensional nature of culture, especially with the central concern of this book in mind – the interaction of culture and Christian faith in today's context. From what has already been seen, what aspects appear essential for any description of 'culture'?

1. It is a uniquely human creation or product, a way of adapting to the world that distinguishes human beings from animals. As such it is an embodiment of human freedom and transcendence.

2. It is something inherited from the past, and yet it changes and adapts in order to cope with different moments of history and of geography.

3. It evolves into a selective set of assumptions, often uncon-

sciously assimilated within a given group or society. Thus culture has an enormous impact on the quality and tone of religious faith.

4. Culture involves an entire way of life shared by people; as such it can be a source of solidarity and identity.

5. Underlying this social manifestation culture is found to involve a convergence of both visible factors and acquired ways of interpreting the world.

6. For instance, culture carries and expresses:
   (a) meanings and beliefs (or visions of life);
   (b) values (norms for behaviour);
   (c) customs, practices and traditions (patterns of response).

7. Cultural expressions may frequently embody themselves in institutions and systems (which preserve those meanings and values) or in symbolic forms (a flag, forms of ritual etc.).

8. The field of culture ranges from everyday routines and responses to larger explorations of the significance and worth of existence. Indeed different layers often converge in one simple act: eating together serves both nutrition and a sense of belonging.[38]

9. At its 'higher' reaches, culture includes not only such spiritual activities as art or literature, but some ultimately religious vision.

10. By its nature culture is self-communicating, seeking to pass on its cumulative wisdom to future generations; this aspect runs into difficulty during periods of rapid change of social forms.

11. Since they are historical products, shaped by complex political influences, cultures are fallible constructs, in need of constant discernment, questioning and renewal.

12. Throughout most of human history, cultures have been rooted in religious consciousness; a central crisis of culture today comes from the split between culture and religion over the last two centuries or so.

That last horizon points towards the next few chapters here, which will deal with the increasing attention to culture by Christian churches today.

Chapter Two

Four Theorists of Change

*[What is] dubious is the general nineteenth century presumption
that modernity adversely affects religion by taking the wonder and
mystery out of the universe – as if religion depends more on the
physical environment than on the quality of social relations.*

(Mary Douglas)[1]

*Technology, like anything else new, must be faced not in a spirit of
nostalgia but in the historical spirit. A kind of cosmic nostalgia, the
desire somehow to escape from history, is an old pagan disease. There
is nothing Christian in it.* (Walter J. Ong)[2]

This chapter offers the reader a synopsis of insights from four
stimulating Catholic thinkers, who reflect on cultural change from
very different perspectives. Mary Douglas is a cultural anthropologist, who did most of her initial fieldwork in Africa in the 1950s,
and particularly in Congo. Author of many books, she has consist-
ently criticised some common assumptions of sociologists on such
issues as secularisation of the pre-modern world. Thus in the best-
known study of her earlier years, *Natural Symbols: Explorations in
Cosmology*, she argues that the contrast of secular with religious
has nothing to do with the contrast of modern with traditional: in
her judgement the idea that primitive people are by nature
religious is untenable. Instead all kinds of 'scepticism, materialism
and spiritual fervour are to be found in the range of tribal
societies'.[3] Therefore she casts doubt on the thesis that secularism
– in the sense of a this-worldly framework that remains within
everyday concerns – is mainly a product of urbanisation or of the
rise of science, or the breakdown of traditional social cohesion.
Instead it is 'an age-old cosmological type, a product of a definable
social experience'.[4]

Differences between cultures, according to Douglas, are rooted in how people learn to perceive their social relationships with one another. In this regard four factors are mutually reinforcing: the acquired ways of perceiving one's place in society, the social context and its dominant patterns of interaction, individual behaviour choices, and the forms of religious vision typical of different cultures. A child starts by assimilating the social assumptions of the 'tribe', and thus gradually the self comes to view the surrounding world with a particular slant, which in turn shapes his or her typical expectations of others. Thus people live certain implicit choices and these form a shared common sense that seems natural but in fact is a product of a certain way of being together. The tone and quality of these relationships in turn influence the kind of religious horizon likely within a given culture. Douglas insists on a cultural analysis that gives pride of place to the individual's way of responding to the surrounding world, but in addition she stresses the connection between these different perceptions of the self in society with various forms of religious or non-religious visions of existence. How the individual experiences these interactions involves an implicit choice concerning what Douglas calls a cosmology.

She is especially known for her four models of cultural difference and of how the variations between different social contexts and cosmologies can be understood in terms of what she calls 'grid' and 'group'. This is a flexible but simple way of describing how people live with different built-in interpretative schemes of how to act in relation to others. It provides a method of categorising cultural differences and cultural change. It also helps to show how cultural categories, far from being autonomous from social relationships, are always influenced by social situations. Culture and society in this presentation can never be divorced, nor can one of them dominate the other totally. Here I shall seek to explain the fourfold typology of cultures in order to suggest how this model casts light on the contemporary situation of culture and faith.

'Group' refers to forms of top-down authority and pressure on the individual exercised by society: allegiance to the group leadership is central here. Where 'group' is strong, conformity and obedience are key influences, and people tend to be classified as members or not, as either insiders or outsiders.

'Grid' refers to a less controlling and less explicit form of organis-ation, constituted by the horizontal network of roles, rules and relationships that people build up with one another. 'Grid' is both more informal and more complex than 'group', focusing on the self rather than on the collectivity. Hence 'grid' is less a question of social control from above than of assumptions that guide how individuals behave towards one another in different situations. By putting the two wavelengths of social organisation together, Douglas shows how society can move from highly structured to highly unstructured situations, not only in terms of social obedi-ence (group) but also in terms of interpersonal expectations (grid). She advances the thesis that the resulting four forms of organis-ation (with all kinds of inner nuances depending on the position on a graph) are at the root of how cultural forms have an influ-ence on religion. In her words there is a 'dependence of the form of religion on the form of organization'.[5] As in her own presen-tations of this group grid theory, it is best understood with the aid of a diagram.

The vertical line represents the range of 'grid' influence, from zero presence at the bottom to strongest at the top. Similarly the horizontal line represents the range of 'group' control, from zero at the left to strongest at the right. In this way four squares emerge from the different possible combinations of grid and group, thus offering a flexible model for identifying four quite different cultural formations. As Douglas has written, 'culture is nothing if not a collective product',[6] and she approaches it through the different patterns or fields of relationships that make up a community.

Starting with the top right square – position 'A' – one has what could be called traditional culture, where both grid and group are strong. Such a culture involves a combination of clear authority, a hierarchy that commands group life, with a network of implicit norms that structure interaction between individuals. Stability and dependency are features of such a culture. Religiously there is usually a strong sense of divine transcendence, celebrated through set rituals, and further reinforced through fear of divine punish-ment for any transgression against loyalty to the community (group) or against the accepted rules that govern interpersonal behaviour (grid). It has been argued that the typical 'Catholic

TYPES OF CULTURES

GRID
strong = network of assumptions/rules
guiding behaviour of individuals,
shared social expectations

'B'
self at centre,
competitive individualism,
market-exchange relationships,
materialist symbols of status

'A'
order/balance of hierarchical
society,
sense of belonging + stable
relationships with others

GROUP
weak

GROUP
strong = allegiance,
control,
conformity,
pressure on individuals

'C'
isolated individuals,
no structures, supports or
fixed roles,
transitory relations,
secularist horizon

'D'
'sect'-style collectivity,
authoritarian regime,
fundamentalism,
strict separation of
insiders/outsiders

GRID
weak

culture' of the decades before Vatican II was of this tightly ordered kind.[7] But there is no need to interpret this 'A' square as automatically a domineering or unhappy culture. In fact within this square there can be flexible and humane forms of authority and secure social roles: when this happens, this culture offers a set of supports for the individual that most people are looking for, even today. It is the natural culture that throughout the ages has provided a home for human beings and given them a religious cosmology with which to confront the dilemmas of existence.

The shift from the top right to the top left-hand square is one way of understanding the major cultural movement that leads from a stable culture where religion is part of the fabric of life to a more free-floating and individualist culture where the language of religion undergoes severe challenge. In the understanding of Mary Douglas, a culture without 'group' allegiance but with high 'grid' interaction is essentially a competitive society rooted in exchange relationships of a quasi-commercial kind. The sense of belonging to a definite group lessens but 'ego-centred categories of behaviour' are at a maximum.[8] Role definition does not come any longer from some collective authority but rather from gaining recognition in a competitive market with other individuals. The appearance of success becomes important, and one is reminded of the conflict at the heart of Jane Austen's novels, between a traditional ethic of objective virtue and the more subjectivist behaviour that Austen satirises as connected with city life.

As loyalty to the group diminishes, a more individualist status-seeking becomes central: the curbs on this more ego-based culture that were present in square 'A' lessen dramatically in square 'B', simply because individual interaction ('grid') now monopolises the field, without the balancing influence of social responsibility ('group'). Relationships and alliances become fragile and temporary. With a decline of group identity and of a sense of belonging, a culture becomes more pluralistic, more pragmatic and more materialist in its symbols of success. Self-interest is a principal driving force behind individual choices and behaviour. In such a culture even religious forms become more ego-based. God is less a revelation to be obeyed than a source of peace and comfort for the self. Thus in what Douglas describes as 'a distinctive culture of competitive individualism', the tendency is to foster 'personal religion'.[9] Typical of this context is that religion is privatised and called upon to meet people's needs for self-fulfilment. This inevitably entails a certain secularisation of religion, even if a fuller form of secularism is more likely to be found in square 'C'.

It is not hard to recognise many aspects of urban 'modernity' in what Douglas describes as low-group and strong-grid, but her analysis puts the emphasis less on the external situation of a city than on the changing place of the self within the social organisation. When one moves to the bottom left square, one finds a more extreme (perhaps 'postmodern') lack of structures and supports. Here role definition is at a minimum, since there are pressures from neither the 'group' nor the 'grid'. Relationships become even more optional and mobile. Whereas in 'B' there was a certain community of competition, in 'C' isolation and lack of communication between people are typical features. Everything is optional, as exemplified in 'modern industrial society [where] there are probably more opportunities to live as an isolate than ever'.[10] She cites the example of a girl working at a cash checkpoint in a supermarket as a summary of this culture of minimum grid and minimum group pressures: within the patterns of such a job there is practically no opportunity to relate to people or to have any sense of belonging.

From the point of view of religion, if a certain reductiveness of faith to individual needs was characteristic of 'B', in 'C' secularist indifference becomes dominant. If the main form of unbelief in 'A' is an opting out of the structures of belonging (for instance, from church practice), and if in 'B' the tendency is to reject God as irrelevant to my life, in 'C' the very question of some ultimate meaning and spiritual horizon fades into silence or unreality. The first impression of this square of structureless existence is that it is a disaster area for Christian faith, where the sense of wonder shrivels up and there is no longer any language for speaking of the mystery of God. However, at least one religious commentator offers a much more positive reading of this cultural situation: it is so lacking in structures that it is free to build 'intentional Christian communities' creatively and from below. This interpretation assumes that the very absence of control from group or grid is a cultural blessing, where personal identity will come 'from an awareness of one's self-worth and potential for change', and hence it provides fertile ground for counter-cultural communities to grow.[11]

This may be true for some people, but on average this empty space seems more likely to lead to a certain cultural desolation, where drifting dominates and where lack of supports leaves people without any scaffolding for an encounter with religious revelation. Moreover, insofar as today's cultural situation in much of the Western world leaves people isolated along the line of the 'C' square, a frequent result seems to be an anchorless form of spiritual searching of the New Age variety. The absence of pressures may provoke creative freedom and rediscovery of the gospel for some, but a more probable outcome – one that is increasingly verified in the comfortable post-industrial world – is a return of gnostic credulity without any contact with the traditional wisdom of the Churches. In other words, without some belonging to a 'group' or some community links with the 'grid' of other people, the typical cultural form of religiousness can easily become secularised, unchurched, narcissistic and lonely.

Square 'D' represents a radically different response to the complexity of today, the conservative tendency to close the doors of dialogue between faith and culture, a stance of distance and of negative judgement against the dominant values around, and ultimately a return of religious fundamentalism. Douglas would not necessarily agree with giving labels to the previous three squares: nevertheless, 'A' is largely pre-modern, 'B' summarises many ills of modernity, and 'C' seems to include many of the elements of the 'postmodern'. If so, then 'D' represents the reaction on behalf of various religious groups today to withdraw into highly structured fortresses of resistance to the chaos that they perceive in late modernity and postmodernity.

In studying the 'weak grid/strong group' form of culture, which Douglas has on different occasions called the 'enclave' or the 'sect' model, she stresses the desire to insulate the tight group from the surrounding world and the low priority given to horizontal relationships between people ('grid'). Allegiance to authority is all, and is often accompanied by a rigid asceticism concerning pleasure or non-conformity of any kind. Such a situation of dependency is one into which a newborn baby always comes, but when imposed on adults it entails a danger of authoritarianism that discourages any individual creativity or freedom.

Dramatic and extreme examples of this 'D' culture are provided by the various tragedies involving religious sects in recent years: the mass suicides in different countries or the bombing of the Tokyo underground. But Douglas would see this cultural form embodied in any situation where collectivism outweighs individual choices and imposes various roles on its members. This kind of group often presents itself to itself as egalitarian but in reality this entails an absence of scope for individual initiative. Another self-image is as a dissenting minority and this goes hand in hand with a certain suspicion towards non-members. As Douglas remarks concerning all types of culture, 'Paradoxically the greatest source of strength for entrenching a particular cultural bias is the mutual hostility between cultures.'[12] This comment seems particularly true for the preservation of group identity in this sectarian form of culture.

Standing back from the details of this fourfold diagram, one should stress that it is a question of understanding the silent pressures of different cultural contexts on the individual and hence on the possibility of arriving at religious commitment. In the words of Mary Douglas, 'Decisions are difficult to reach. They rest on tacit assumptions, not on argued syllogisms.' And she adds that the social organisation that comes to seem natural in different cultures constitutes a particular 'path' of decision-making for the members of that culture. 'This is the central argument of cultural theory: culture itself is constrained' by its own 'different logical base' and this can help to explain 'how any type of collective can resist pressures to transform'.[13] The great advantage of her grid/ group model is to have clarified different forms of base and bias in diverse cultures, of their mutual resistance and conflict, and of their divergent assumptions and priorities. She shows how underlying visions and beliefs, rooted in various forms of social expectation and control, produce four completely different forms of culture. Although she identified these conflicting forms of cultural environment in 'primitive' tribes, her insights are of considerable relevance for understanding our present cultural shifts and indeed the misunderstandings that can arise between different sub-cultures within Christianity today.

The issue of cultural agency

More briefly, and by way of contrast to Mary Douglas, we can draw upon another British expert on the interaction of society and culture. The sociologist Margaret Archer explores how people feel both imprisoned by culture and yet able to resist its pressures. With the aim of describing how cultural transformation comes about, she rejects any image of culture as a neatly coherent ethos or 'symbolically consistent universe'; instead of being such an all-inclusive web, culture is a 'shapeless, seething and shifting thing'.[14] Her analysis of this mobility within culture is grounded in a distinction between a 'Cultural System' and the 'Socio-Cultural' domain. The system coincides with the 'ideas' that hold sway within any given society (and hence is loosely parallel to 'group' for Douglas). By contrast, the socio-cultural structure has to do with lived interactions between people (and hence similar to 'grid'). In Archer's view, whenever one finds 'high Socio-Cultural integration' as a way of life, this is more influential than an imposed belief system: 'Culture is *not* always shared because it is binding but may sometimes be *binding because shared*.'[15]

Her theory of change (or 'morphogenesis') involves a complicated analysis of possible ways in which 'culture' and 'structure' influence one another. 'Culture', in the sense of the beliefs that dominate a society, can be either static or in ferment. 'Structure', in the sense of interest groups that hold power, can also be firmly established or else in conflict. Hence, if 'ideational control' goes hand in hand with unchallenged structural domination one has a very traditionalist society, but this is not often the case in the contemporary world. Sometimes the push for transformation begins on the level of 'culture' and sometimes on the level of 'structure'. Thus the Enlightenment started on the level of ideas and then had an impact on the political shape of society. Similarly, the Scientific Revolution was initially intellectual; the Industrial Revolution was more a social phenomenon influencing work patterns and causing rapid urbanisation.

In spite of the inevitable limitations of any culture – due to place, language, education and so on – Archer wants to stress that a different future can be forged through forms of cultural 'agency', due to the 'reflective ability of human beings to fight back against their conditioning'.[16] Even from this brief account of some of her insights, it is clear that she offers not just analytical models of change but a powerful argument that although cultural transformation is highly complex, it is still possible to counteract the dominant culture and to help create alternative forms of life.

Walter Ong: oral vs print cultures

The work of Walter J. Ong offers a complementary perspective for
these insights from anthropology and sociology. The background
of this American Jesuit lies in literary criticism and in theology;
his special field of interest over many years is the significance of
the shifts in our ways of human communication – moving from
oral cultures to the writing and printing revolutions and then to
the electronic media of today. These three major evolutions were
brought about by technological developments, and in each case
the arrival of new technology had a major impact on culture itself.
When, for instance, writing ousted the patterns of an older oral
culture, it 'transformed human consciousness', introducing 'division and alienation' but also 'highly interiorized stages of
consciousness'.[17] Then a different phase of thinking arrived, when
printing allowed knowledge to be localised in visual space – as
distinct from the essentially communal and present-tense communication typical of 'orality'. The eye took over from the ear as
the chief contact with reality.

Moreover, all these cultural developments presented challenges
for the mediation of religious faith. Whereas sound is 'related to
present actuality rather than to past or future', and is 'a special
sensory key to interiority',[18] the new dominance of the visual
caused a depersonalisation of culture and indeed a privatisation
of religion. From a theological point of view, Ong is a great
defender of the human values of 'orality', without ever falling into
the nostalgia of regretting subsequent cultural wavelengths (or
idealising a less literate past). Faith comes from hearing, according
to St Paul. In Ong's view the sound of the spoken word is an
avenue into the interior of the other person. Printed communication is much more distant and impersonal by comparison. Indeed
the 'decay of dialogue', that was one of the indirect effects of the
invention of the printing press, constituted a radically different
context for the communication of faith. Print makes reality private
and seemingly controllable whereas 'the spoken word moves from
interior to interior' and genuine interpersonal encounter is
'achieved largely through voice'.[19]

What Mary Douglas saw in the shift from more traditional to

more individualist societies, Walter Ong associated with the visual-isation of reality caused by the cultural revolution inaugurated by the technology of writing and of its later developments – book culture and printing. 'Writing seals off its product from direct dialogue: the writer creates his text in isolation'; as in the case of Douglas' interpretation of the move into 'B', a certain lonely individualism results.[20] When human communication loses its quality of encounter and of direct relationship, thinking itself undergoes a subtle change and human consciousness is restruc-tured in its sense of the real. When a print mentality dominates, we tend to desire 'closure' or certitude of a visible and verifiable kind. In this cultural situation, the truth of religious revelation can be dismissed as insufficiently objective and its nature as a relational and spoken Word remain neglected. In this sense print culture is one of the gateways to the empirical science that seemed the only conceivable kind during modernity.

What Ong calls 'oral-aural' culture (because it involves both a speaking and a listening) is much more existentially real than the strange act of reading in silence. When he turns his attention to the twentieth century, Ong becomes enthusiastic about the poten-tials of a 'secondary orality', caused by yet another technological development that again is having enormous impact on human consciousness: the world of electronic communications – especially radio and television – has retrieved the lost dimension of voice. This development is capable of healing some of the cultural imbal-ances caused by the impersonal world of print. It is not a question of returning to the 'primary orality' of preliterate cultures but of a new contact with personal interiority and mystery, and hence with the question of God. What printed visualisation tended to neglect, this new orality makes possible again. Its relational quality not only leaves room for faith but fosters the human capacities for interpersonal hearing where the Word can enter. Thus as distinct from the 'closed fields of systems' of print, now there is a fresh openness 'connected with our new kind of orality, the secondary orality of our electronic age'.[21] The new culture is fascinated with interconnections and with personal interiority. It values diversity and convergence thinking. It repersonalises the world that printing had made reductively 'spatial'. This second orality also values the present moment whereas writing tends to remove life from time.

In Ong's view of cultural history, offered here in a necessarily compressed form, the arrival of writing and of printing marks a crucial dividing line in history. He sees its overall impact as questionable and ambiguous, especially during the period of modernity. But if we are integrating orality into culture again, an excessive focus on private and visual reading may give way to a more interpersonal sense of encounter. This will be one of the many strands of postmodernity and of its possibly greater openness to the religious dimension.

René Girard: the shadows of culture

A fourth and quite different perspective on change can be taken from the writings of René Girard. This French-born literary scholar become anthropologist and even theologian is famous for his challenging theory of culture as rooted in violence. Leaving aside some of his debatable arguments about the origins of human history and sacrifice, these few paragraphs try to show how his thought casts light on our theme of faith and culture. Girard would see Christian faith (to which he returned at the age of 35 after years of atheism) as radically counter-cultural but not simply as a critique of the ills of our world. For him all human cultures are infected with a spirit of rivalry between human beings. He sees the biblical figure of Cain as 'the founder of the first culture'.[22] More often than not, our cultural identities are born from being 'against' those who are not of our tribe or outlook. Girard's other fundamental discovery is what he calls the 'mimetic triangle' – a process that came to light through his study of novels and was later confirmed in his explorations in anthropology and in the Bible. The triangle thesis is that our desires are always indirect: I want something, not in itself, but because someone else has it. In fact envy always taints and twists my desires. 'Mimetic', from the Greek for imitation, means that we learn everything – from language to life-values – from echoing others. Hence culture is a huge school of imitation, and if it is dominated by a spirit of enmity, then it becomes a school of collective violence. Culture, in this sense, is born from scapegoating the victims of history and it continues to foster those attitudes of power and hostility. This 'conflictual mimesis' is 'contagious' and is capable of obsessing an 'entire community'.[23] Obviously this portrayal of culture is far from the ideal and humanising source of development found in Enlightenment thinkers. In Girard's view culture is shadowed from the beginning and remains secretly addicted to hostility. In similar fashion another French thinker, Michel de Certeau, insists that culture can conceal conflict and, until its essentially plural and everyday nature is recognised, it can give the illusion of social cohesion.[24]

Against dangerous self-images lurking in the culture, Girard sees the biblical vision as a force of resistance and salvation. The voice of the victim sounds with increasing eloquence through the pages of the Old Testament: from the gentleness of God with Abel to the cries of Job to the extraordinary trust of the suffering servant songs in Isaiah. But only in the unique drama of the gospels do we find the total unmasking and overturning of the culture of rivalry. Jesus is so utterly beyond that logic of hostility that he disturbs all cultural assumptions: he becomes the victim of all hate because he is all love. This counter-cultural crisis changes culture for ever and from within. 'In the Gospels we have the revelation of the mechanism that dominates culture unconsciously.'[25] Through this revelation we are set free from culture's dark inheritance and become free to live out another vision of who we are and who we can be. Our desires can liberate themselves from distorted self-images and from mechanisms of suspicion. What a famous medieval book calls the 'imitation of Christ' takes on new meaning and offers hope for a culture that places compassion above victimising. 'Following Christ means giving up mimetic desire', or rather the form of it that keeps us prisoners, and sharing the desire of Christ himself.[26] The adventure of Christian faith is to heal culture of its hidden logic of violence (often sacralised and performed in the name of religion). In Christ we unlearn the rivalry that dominates history and we slowly learn another language of 'positive mimesis'.

The conversion of culture in Girard's vision is what church texts call 'evangelisation of culture' but his interpretation is more penetrating and provocative than anything found in official statements on that theme. In the words of one of Girard's best theological commentators, we grow up culturally as 'conflictual little animals, with a built-in mechanism for shoring up our fragile identity', but into this tragic landscape comes the self-giving of God 'enabling us to become receivers rather than graspers'. This transformation stems from 'the new cultural reality inaugurated by the death and resurrection of Christ'.[27] Girard claims that in today's world a new concern for victims 'dominates the total planetary culture in which we live'.[28] This clearly controversial thinker invites us to ponder cultural change at a more radically religious level than the bland explorations of secular sociology.

Chapter Three

A Major Theme of Vatican II

The meaning of Vatican II was the acknowledgement of history.

(Bernard Lonergan)[1]

The central non-ecclesiological issue at the Second Vatican Council and in the Post-Conciliar Church is the relationship between faith and culture. (Dermot Lane)[2]

The Second Vatican Council initiated a whole new wavelength for Roman Catholic understanding of culture. It was the first time in church history that an ecumenical council debated at length on such an issue and then devoted a substantial chapter to this theme in *Gaudium et Spes*, the Pastoral Constitution dealing with the Church in the Modern World. Although this chapter was considerably longer than the three sections dealing with atheism, in the years immediately after the Council, great attention was given to the issue of atheism, and only gradually – from the mid-seventies onwards – have cultural concerns come to the centre of the stage. In this chapter the aim is to outline the significance of the Vatican II stance on culture; the one following will examine later developments in Catholic thinking in this area.

The story of the surprising birth of *Gaudium et Spes* has often been told, and needs only a brief summary here. It was an unexpected child of the Council: at the outset the proposed texts, prepared by the Roman Curia, remained within the mould of an old-fashioned theology – defensive, deductive, neo-scholastic and ahistorical. Moreover, the topics were all 'ad intra', dealing with ecclesial issues such as liturgy or the Church's sense of its own identity. At an early stage of the three-year period of the Council, the Bishops voted to jettison the prepared drafts and to start their reflections from a significantly different basis. This was an indication of the minor revolution that marked the Council, which embodied itself in two new priorities: opting for a return to the roots of revelation as a source of renewal, and for a more positive and inductive listening to the situations of today as 'signs of the times'. In the light of the incarnation, history could be reread as the carrier of mystery. Such a stance, combining spiritual and pastoral approaches, ousted the entrenched attitudes of intellectualism and negative judgements against modern culture. It also gave birth to a new wavelength of conciliar language, one that sought to describe rather than to judge, and to do so in ways that would make sense to non-theologians.

In the early sessions of the Council there was practically no attention to the 'modern world' in itself, and it was only when the Council had been underway for more than a year that the proposal was made to devote time and effort to discerning today's context for faith, the world 'ad extra', beyond the confines of Church. In the words of Cardinal Suenens it was time for the Church to perform 'an act of charity towards the world'.[3] Largely under his influence *Gaudium et Spes* came into being – a long document that can be viewed as an essay in theological anthropology on contemporary culture, and where one chapter, representing about a tenth of the whole text, is devoted to the topic of culture.

In this context it is assumed that the text will be easily available to the reader. Hence these pages offer a guide to the main issues. The key definition or description is as follows (No. 53 – in my own translation):

> It is one of the marks of the human person to reach true and authentic humanity only through culture, that is, by cultivating natural gifts and values. Whenever human life is involved, nature and culture are intimately connected.
>
> In its general sense the word 'culture' stands for everything by which human beings refine and develop their various capacities of mind and body. It includes efforts to control the cosmos by knowledge or by work, as well as ways of humanizing social life within the family or civic community through the progress of customs and institutions.

It is significant that it begins by relating culture to the nature of the human person and by claiming that only through culture does a person arrive at authentic humanity. Immediately two foundation stones of Catholic thinking on culture become clear: that culture is intimately linked with the dignity of the person and with the call of freedom to become more fully human. These are notes that will sound again and again in Catholic commentaries of later decades.

Having established this basic perspective on culture, the text goes on to a more detailed description of what culture means. What is notable here is that the Council openly recognises a shift in the understanding of culture today and indeed it balances three levels of meaning – the older sense of culture as self-cultivation, a more phenomenological or anthropological view of culture as embodied in a whole range of social systems and expressions, and thirdly, an explicit recognition of the plurality of cultures.

At first the conciliar statement lists five dimensions of human development, three of which (1, 4, 5) belong within the classical meaning of culture, while the remaining two (2, 3) come from a more sociological understanding of culture and indicate concrete ways in which human development embodies itself in social realities:

1. cultivating one's intellectual and physical gifts (this intrapersonal sense of culture summarises the more traditional meaning of the word);
2. mastery of the earth through research and through work (here the Council intends to include the modern spheres of science and technology);
3. efforts to humanise society and family life by means of traditions and institutions (this covers evolution in such areas as politics, education, health and all the complex factors that create modern societies);
4. spiritual self-expression of the great human hopes (thus joining the world of art to the world of religious faith);
5. preserving and communicating inspiring visions of life for the 'progress' of humankind (this touches on culture as transmission of values from the past to the future).

Having mingled these characteristics of humanistic and empirical culture, the Council turns to another specifically modern interpretation. Stating explicitly that it is considering the 'historical and social' dimensions of culture, it adds that contemporary sociology and anthropology bring to light a 'plurality of cultures'. It then gives a list of reasons why different 'styles of living' and 'scales of value' exist: these are grounded in differences in work patterns, in religious worldviews, in ways of self-expression, as well as in social structures or institutions. In short, the Council in a few short sentences moves from the traditional or 'high' view of culture as self-transcendence to two newer horizons: the sense of culture as involving living conditions, social organisations and assumptions, and an acknowledgement of the different forms of life that account for cultural diversity throughout history.

Thus, this paragraph 53 links the older meaning of culture – as a field of human growth and of intellectual or aesthetic achievement – with the more empirical sense of culture (or cultures) as embodied in social structures and in historically diverse approaches to life. This key section of *Gaudium et Spes* ends by noting that each human community, with its specific history and geography, has its own inheritance of wisdom and its own way of fostering basic human values; hence, even if not stated openly, it is evident that there can be no 'uncultured' nations and the monopoly exercised by the more aristocratic meaning of culture has been broken for good.

The remainder of the chapter on culture is neatly divided into three named sub-sections with three paragraphs within each section. The first section deals with the contemporary cultural context, the second with principles of cultural development, and the third with responsibilities of believers in the cultural field. For present purposes, it will be enough to touch on some of the main topics that arise, especially those that will continue to be central in Catholic reflection on culture in later decades. Each paragraph can be given a quick title, sometimes echoing the official headings in the text, followed by a short account of the key points.

A radically different context.   Paragraph 54 speaks of a 'new age of human history', where social changes have brought about a 'mass culture' that has enormous impact on how people think and act. Interestingly, this paragraph is couched in a deliberately descriptive tone, with no hint of negative judgement concerning mass culture; indeed, it expresses a hope that these new conditions can build a more 'universal' culture, expressing the 'unity' of humankind, and yet respecting the 'particular features' of local cultures.

Historical and cultural consciousness. Paragraph 55, with a title speaking of humanity as 'author of culture', moves on to speak of 'a new humanism being born' in today's world. This involves a deeper awareness of 'autonomy and responsibility' felt by people today before the task of building up 'their community's culture'. Again this characteristic is seen in a very positive light as indicating 'spiritual and moral maturity' before the calls of history.

Honest facing of dangers. As if admitting that the previous two paragraphs might be excessively optimistic, paragraph 56 lists some of the contradictions and ambiguities in contemporary culture, but it does so through a series of questions, thus avoiding any appearance of condemnation or criticism. These questions raise such issues as the danger of new cultural forms undermining traditional wisdom, how to reconcile specialisation with a capacity for wonder, or how to prevent 'legitimate autonomy of culture' becoming narrowly secularist and anti-religious.

Cultural tasks in the light of faith. Paragraph 57 is the first of three devoted to a more specifically theological understanding of the whole field of culture, and this first paragraph situates the calls of culture within the overall vocation of Christians. The final destiny of life with God should energise rather than diminish the engagement of believers in the humanisation of this world. Hence cultural activities are central to the Christian calling. The text goes on to admit that the impact of science and technology can narrow one's sense of truth and produce a false self-sufficiency, but it immediately denies that such ills follow from contemporary culture itself. Once again there is a deliberate effort to evaluate modern culture as a bearer of 'positive values', which can prepare people for the gospel message and even be grounded in divine love.

Relationship between gospel and culture. If the previous paragraph dealt with faith and culture, this shifts the focus to gospel and

culture. In view of our subsequent chapter here on the work of the
World Council of Churches, it is worth noting that even the order
of presentation of these two sections seems significant. Faith-and-
culture will remain a principal category for Catholic reflection in
later decades and it raises issues of responding creatively to this
particular moment of human history in the light of faith. Gospel-
and-culture, however, will be the preferred expression at the heart
of WCC explorations, and, as will be seen, it raises a rather different
set of concerns about how gospel revelation can be expressed in
different cultures. In broad terms (as will be seen later), Catholic
underlying assumptions seem more anthropological and philosophical, whereas the WCC priorities seem more evangelical and
socio-political.

Paragraph 58 begins by evoking the cultural nature of revelation
itself, where God's progressive self-communication adapted itself
to the culture of different ages. Against this background it unites
two perspectives concerning evangelisation (without using that
word which entered Catholic discourse from the mid-seventies on):
that the gospel message transcends all cultures, purifying and
transforming them, and yet the mission of the Church is to embody
the gospel in different cultures, enriching the culture and being
herself enriched in the process. The revelation of God, not being a
magic power but a word entrusted to humanity, needs constant
communication in new situations and this naturally entails cultural
sensitivity. This is a basis for what will later be called inculturation.

In addition this paragraph contains the important assertion that
the Church has no fixed relationship with any culture: this is
in the spirit of an eloquent speech of Cardinal Lercaro during the
Council debate, when he argued that the Church should embrace
a certain cultural poverty, not clinging to the riches of the past even
in thought systems or artistic expressions; while always rooted in
Scripture, the Church should explore the languages of contemporary culture and its emerging values. New credibility and
religious force would be found from such humility, according to
Lercaro.

Rightful autonomy of culture. Paragraph 59 comments on conditions necessary to ensure the authentic development of culture.

Culture flows from a person's rational and social nature and should defend the human person and serve the good of the community. Therefore it is called to foster wonder and awareness on different levels – religious, moral and social. But in order to safeguard these ideal goals of culture, its legitimate independence needs to be recognised – including liberty of research, expression and information. Above all, culture has the right not to be manipulated by those in power.

The remaining three paragraphs are more practical in focus and indeed some of the positions already seem dated or over-cautious in expression.

The right to culture.   Paragraph 60 speaks of making cultural benefits available to all. On the level of 'basic culture', there are problems such as illiteracy, or conditions of life or work that are dehumanising. Ideally all should have the opportunity to develop themselves, and in this context the document refers to women sharing fully in cultural life. Underlying this paragraph is the assumption that cultural 'goods' are not just a luxury for the rich, but something essential to all human life. The implicit philosophy is that because self-development is a duty of each person's human freedom, access to cultural opportunities is a right.

The difficulty of cultural synthesis today.   Paragraph 61 recognises that because of the complexity and specialisation of different fields of culture, it is increasingly rare to be able to achieve an organic vision of life. Opportunities for education and for leisure have greatly expanded, but an 'integral culture' will not come about without a certain quality of reflective questioning and some grasp of the crucial relevance of culture for the growth of the person.

The role of culture in Christian formation.   Paragraph 62 is the last and longest of the whole chapter on culture and bears the marks of being something of a dustbin for ideas that did not fit in easily in other parts of the text. Nevertheless it has a certain coherence and unity, which focuses on the issue of the relations between the Church and culture: it acknowledges tensions and shadows in different moments of history, but commits the Church to a constant dialogue with new forms of thought and art. This hope is grounded in the trust that truth cannot ultimately be contradictory and that fields of knowledge have their own autonomy. It is worth remarking that although many asked for explicit mention of the Galileo case in this context, it had been referred to in an earlier paragraph of *Gaudium et Spes* (36) and hence was not mentioned again here. However, the text does take account of a gap between artists and the Church in modern times; it calls for an acknowledgement of new forms of art and encourages their presence in places of worship.

Among other important themes mentioned here are the following: an openness to new vistas in contemporary thinking in order to be able to discern new developments in the light of faith; the need for interdisciplinary work in theology; encouragement for lay people to study theology; the need for freedom of expression by experts in various fields.

Conclusion

Reading this chapter of Vatican II nearly forty years later, a number of points call for comment. First, this text has proved prophetic: even if during the Council it was not one of the more dramatic developments, with the passing of time its significance has grown and indeed the theme of culture has become quite central in the thinking of Pope John Paul II. Second, some of these statements of the Council now seem innocently optimistic in their approach: this was due to a deliberate option on the part of the Council to avoid condemnations and to give a sympathetic pastoral reading of the modern situation. Third, many of the key issues treated in this chapter continued to be central in the decades ahead, and hence church reflection concerning culture still looks back to *Gaudium et Spes* as its *magna charta*. This will become obvious in our next section dealing with post-conciliar Catholic developments in this field and in particular with the extraordinary prominence given to culture by Pope John Paul II.

Chapter Four

Catholic Developments since 1965

American culture is desperate for a conversation about public issues set in a moral framework . . . Encourage that conversation, build a sense of community that flows from your practice and your conviction that Catholics and ideas are not a contradiction in terms.

(Margaret O'Brien Steinfels)[1]

The central debate of our time has switched increasingly from politics and economics to culture. (Michael Novak)[2]

The changing role of culture in official Catholic approaches since 1965 can be told in two parts. One is like a brief prologue: it concerns the 1974 Synod of Bishops on evangelisation and the resulting text of Pope Paul VI entitled *Evangelii nuntiandi* (1975) which deals in part with 'evangelization of culture'. The second part will summarise the enormous amount of attention given to culture since John Paul II was elected Pope in 1978, and will try to identify the principal lines of reflection that have emerged during this period.

A more confrontative approach

It is sometimes claimed that *Evangelii nuntiandi* is the most important of post-conciliar papal documents and the one that has had the most lasting impact. Coming as it did exactly ten years after the end of the Council, this 'apostolic exhortation' is couched in an unusually energetic style for such an official text. From the outset it voices an urgency about how the 'hidden energy of the Good News' can find 'evangelical force capable of really transforming the people of this century' (No. 4). It identifies evangelisation as 'the essential mission of the Church' (No. 14), and the source of her identity. It also asserts that the Church remains always in need of being 'evangelized by constant conversion and renewal, in order to evangelize the world with credibility' (No. 15). All this is the context within which Pope Paul arrives at the first major ecclesial statement concerning 'evangelization of culture'.

Just prior to paragraph 20 which is devoted entirely to this topic, evangelisation itself is described as 'bringing the Good News into all the strata of humanity and through its influence transforming humanity from within' (No. 18). The next paragraph focuses on the implications of these different 'strata', insisting that it involves 'affecting and as it were upsetting, through the power of the Gospel, mankind's criteria of judgement, determining values, points of interest, lines of thought, sources of inspiration and models of life, which are in contrast with the Word of God' (No. 19). Thus the evangelisation in question will seek to change the cultural assumptions of people: the implication is that the dominant criteria of common sense are often in silent conflict with the gospel. If so, then evangelisation has to include a new and ambitious goal – the Christian transformation of culture in its many senses.

The relevant section entitled 'evangelization of cultures' can be found in the 'anthology' chapter here. Its key points can be paraphrased as follows:

1.   To transform cultures means going to the roots and not being content with surface appearance.

2.   The gospel is independent of cultures but the Kingdom it proclaims has to be lived by people within their cultural realities; hence the gospel is not incompatible with any culture, in the sense of being able to enter a culture without becoming subject to that culture.

3.   The 'drama of our time' lies in the gap that has opened up between culture and the gospel; healing this split is an essential dimension for evangelisation today.

This tone of anxiety about the ambiguities of contemporary culture was not so present in the texts of Vatican II. Hence this landmark document of a decade later represents a shift in Catholic approaches to culture and one that will continue to have echoes in later years. Culture is taken as a convergence of many layers of significance – as acknowledged in Vatican II – but this complex phenomenon is now discerned religiously as being a potential blockage to the liberating truth of the gospel. By invoking the metaphor of 'drama', this interpretation goes beyond Vatican II and recognises an inevitable conflict in the process of confronting cultures and of transforming them with the vision of the gospel.

A new centrality for culture

The sheer quantity of explorations of culture in the speeches of Pope John Paul II would merit a book in itself, and indeed at least one such book exists in Spanish.[3] For present purposes, however, an overview of key recurring themes will serve in order to identify the principal issues that have emerged in these decades. Obviously there are other sources that could be examined, including the work of the Pontifical Council for Culture – founded by the Pope in 1982 – which produces a quarterly review entitled *Cultures and Faith*. In 1999 this council published a substantial document entitled *Towards a Pastoral Approach to Culture*, which gathers together many of the main official church perspectives and concerns in this area (and which can easily be found on the Internet). However, the principal focus of these pages will be the many discourses of Pope John Paul II on this topic. In order to lighten the presentation, one long quotation of importance will be found in the 'anthology' appendix; and to reduce the number of notes, dates of the speeches will be given in parenthesis in the text.

The personality and the intellectual formation of Karol Wojtyla provide the background for the exceptional emphasis which this Pope has given to culture. With his previous experience in theatre and poetry, his expertise in phenomenological philosophy, his professorship in ethics, his natural tendency is anthropological – approaching even religious issues with a keen sense of the drama of personal meaning and existential choices. But to this humanistic vision, he also brings an acute sense of the spiritual conflict of values at the heart of contemporary history, and hence he views culture as a key zone for the saving of humanity from reductive images of itself.

The American theologian Avery Dulles (now Cardinal) has written an article entitled 'The Prophetic Humanism of John Paul II'. By this he means that Pope Wojtyla (as the Italians often call him) thinks within a certain set of converging concerns: a longing to remind human beings of their potential for self-transcending living in the face of various forms of dehumanisation; a spiritual sense of God's truth because only in harmony with revelation do we find authentic fulfilment; an awareness that each person only discovers his or her genuine humanity through love within community and social solidarity – the opposite of this is 'alienation', a term the Pope borrows from Marx. Dulles has a section on culture which begins as follows:

> Culture has been a major concern of John Paul II from his early days, when he developed his talents for music, poetry and drama. Between 1977 and 1980 he published several important papers on the philosophy of culture . . . The Pope's theory of culture is thoroughly humanistic . . . Everyone lives according to some culture, which determines the mode of one's existence. Culture, as a human achievement, involves our capacity for self-creation, which in turn radiates into the world of products. Culture is a materialization of the human spirit and at the same time a spiritualization of matter. It thus serves to render our world more human.[4]

In his studies of culture prior to his election as Pope, Cardinal Wojtyla stressed the human capacity for spiritual growth through our actions, in particular when they involve relationships of self-giving to others. As early as 1964, in a Polish journal, he argued that a human being needs culture and through culture one creates oneself. In all these years the core of his thinking concerned a philosophy of the human person in the adventure of finding meaning, ultimately the meaning of oneself in Christ. Adapting Marxist terminology in a lecture in Milan in 1977, he spoke of contemplative wonder as the foundation of culture and of how we shape our lives through 'human praxis'. Towards the beginning of that lecture he offered an important distinction concerning the creativity of culture: 'Culture develops principally within . . . the dimension of self-determining subjects. Culture is basically oriented not so much toward the creation of human *products* as toward the creation of the human *self*, which then radiates out into the world of products.' He goes on to borrow from Aquinas in order to distinguish between transitive and intransitive expressions of culture, the former being 'objectified in some product' and the latter having to do with the growth or becoming of the person. In a typical synthesis of his thought, he adds: 'In acting, we not only perform actions, but we also become ourselves, through those actions – we fulfill ourselves in them.'[5] Hence culture has an outer and an inner dimension and Wojtyla seeks to broaden the field of praxis or action in order to acknowledge the primacy of the interior or personal dimension of culture. The transformation of the world is secondary to the transformation of the person. Therefore he rejects any utilitarian reduction of culture to economic production and quotes Kant favourably: 'Act in such a way that the person is always an end and never a means of your action.'[6] Hence for Wojtyla culture is constituted through human praxis in this fuller sense, where people become more truly human, more filled with wonder, and not just where they acquire more means.

Later in the same Milan lecture the discussion of culture moves towards specifically religious and Christian themes, because it is the field where 'the *humanum* encounters the *mysterium*' and where an 'inner communion with truth, goodness, and beauty . . . involves a special radiation of humanity outward'.[7] Finally he moves onto another plane by linking this spiritual approach to culture with the theme of death. We are continually dying, in the sense of the fading away of our 'transitive' products of culture, the more ordinary expressions of praxis. But if it embraces our intransitive dimension of self-transformation, culture transcends the merely external and finds itself 'in battle with death' and defiantly expressing 'our hope of immortality'. Hence we can even speak of 'our continual resurrection in culture'.[8]

In these texts of Wojtyla, prior to his election as Pope, the key to culture lies in a convergence of creativity, spirituality and active commitment in the world, and in this way he proposed a positive view of culture, as an expression of Christian humanism in history and as a witness against the 'existential pessimism' that dominated many cultural expressions of the twentieth century. Interpreting culture in this humanistic and highly spiritual way, Wojtyla unites phenomenology and sociology on the one hand with a creatively Christian interpretation of the person on the other. As will be seen, in his later years as Pope, he retains this fundamental philosophy of culture as crucial to the quality of human living. However, his papal treatments of this theme will move towards another less idealistic view of culture and speak frequently of ordinary or lived culture as immensely influential on people's openness or closedness to faith.

This strong personal interest in the field of culture can be confirmed in more than one statement of the Pope himself. In November 1979, just over a year after his election, he spoke to a special gathering of cardinals, called to reflect with him on major religious issues: 'It will not have escaped your notice that personally I tend to have special interest for the problems of culture, of science and of art.' He went on to voice a claim he repeated on several later occasions: 'In this vital area the destiny of the Church and of the world are at stake in this closing stage of our century' (5.11.79).

In a similar personal vein the Pope said to a meeting of European intellectuals in December 1983: 'You are aware that the theme of culture as such, and even more so the relation between faith and culture, is one that I have pondered much, in the light of my different experiences as a scholar, a Christian, a priest, a bishop, and now as Pope' (16.12.83).

Three versions of culture

When analysing the account of culture offered by *Gaudium et Spes*, we saw that it brought together three main dimensions – humanist, empirical and local. This threefold distinction can serve both to divide and to unify the different ways in which the Pope treats culture. Thus in his many speeches on this theme, it is possible to distinguish three somewhat different meanings for the term 'culture', which we can label creative or humanising culture, sociological or lived culture, and particular or local cultures. Although there is no watertight division between them, nevertheless they point to three significantly different fields of culture.

This can also be illustrated by the frequent practice of John Paul II during his longer visits to various countries. His programme used almost always to include a meeting with 'people of culture', which means the artists, intellectuals, educators and those involved in the world of mass media. This latter world he has described more than once as the primary Areopagus of our contemporary cultural world. His speech to such cultural leaders often evoked the long history of relationship between religion and culture, contrasting this with the present situation, when many forms of culture remain closed within immanence and forgetful of transcendence. If culture is where human beings become more human, and if different cultures represent different ways of facing the question of the meaning of existence, then the whole future of humanity is intimately linked with whatever happens in the field of culture. In short, the Pope's typical call to the world of conscious or creative culture is to realise the high ideals that can guide it and can again shape human wisdom for today. 'Every culture is an effort to ponder the mystery of the world and in particular of the human person: it is a way of giving expression to the transcendent dimension of human life' (United Nations, 5.10.95).

A second use of the term 'culture' in papal discourses focuses rather on lifestyles. If cultivating one's humanity is seen as essentially good (meaning 1) and if local traditions are to be respected for their spiritual depth (meaning 3), living passively within the pressures of modern society is viewed as deceptive and dangerous for basic human values. This meaning of 'culture' as lived assumptions can easily become an 'anti-culture'. The 'dominant culture' is a phrase usually used with negative connotations: 'so much of our dominant culture is a culture of flight from God' (USA, 6.10.95). Occasionally one finds different meanings coming together even in the same sentence: 'A culture that is not at the service of the individual is not a culture' (Peru, 15.5.88). In other words, culture remains an ambiguous human construct, needing constant discernment. The great humanist ideal can fall into self-contradiction, and authentic values of ideal culture are under threat in the actual culture of contemporary secularised societies.

In certain countries and continents the Pope has had meetings with representatives of indigenous or traditional cultures, and here his discourses have normally been both more concrete and more protective. The key message is that the locally inherited wisdom is a rich treasure to be preserved. It should cherish its own values – such as a sense of the sacred or a reverence for the family – and guard them against cultural oppression by more superficial cultural trends (the second sense here). This positive evaluation of minority traditions is occasionally qualified by acknowledgement of potentially ambiguous elements: a passage from the encyclical on missions mentions a danger 'of passing uncritically from a form of alienation from culture to an overestimation of culture. Since culture is a human creation [it] is therefore marked by sin' (*Redemptoris missio*, No. 54).

Foundations for a philosophy of culture

As far as creative or humanistic culture is concerned, the most far-reaching speech of the Pope was that delivered in Paris to the members of UNESCO in June 1980. A few crucial passages from this lengthy speech are given in the 'anthology' at the end of this book. In general it was an impassioned plea to keep the transcendence of the human being at the centre of any approach to culture, and hence not to identify culture only with cultural products or activities. Thus a person's subjective 'being' rather than more externalised 'having' is the source of culture, and the importance of culture is seen best in the light of an integral humanism (that last expression from Jacques Maritain was not used by the Pope but captures well the core of his argument).

With this basic vision, the Pope's presentation elaborated various principles for understanding culture:

1. Taking the human person in his or her 'integrality' means respecting the material and spiritual aspects of humanity; this non-abstract sense of the person in history is the basis for understanding culture.

2. Culture is the key zone where human beings grow into fullness of humanity.

3. The human being is both the subject or shaper of culture and also its object or goal.

4. Historically there has been an 'organic and constitutive link' between religion and culture.

5. Christianity in particular has been a creator of culture because of the value it places on the transcendence of the human person.

6. The primary task of culture is education, not in any narrow sense, but serving spirituality and moral culture.

7. A nation exists through and for its culture, which is sometimes the saviour of its very identity.

It is clear that this is a highly humanistic and philosophical perspective on culture, and such an approach is fundamental for John Paul II. Indeed this particular speech remains a cornerstone of his thinking and is often echoed or quoted by him in later years. Even though this UNESCO discourse builds on the treatment of culture in *Gaudium et Spes* (without ever citing it), it is much more ambitious in its intellectual range. When the Council spoke of humanity being the 'author of culture' (No. 55), it was referring to a new sense of responsibility for history in modern times. When John Paul II speaks of the human person being the subject or architect of culture, he is not thinking of a contemporary sensibility but of something in the very constitution of humanity. More penetratingly than Vatican II, he wants to ground the nature of culture in a reading of human nature as self-transcending. Throughout these years John Paul II offers variations on this metaphysical anthropology of culture, insisting that 'culture is of humanity, by humanity, and for humanity' (10.1.92).

Other key expressions of humanistic culture

With all this background it is clear that the natural bent of John Paul II is to ground his thinking on culture in a philosophy of the human person. Having paused on this UNESCO address, we can summarise later comments on this dimension of culture fairly schematically:

Culture as personal and communal. John Paul II continually insists that culture is 'oriented to the realization of the person in all one's dimensions', but at the same time he stresses that culture belongs to a people: it is the 'particular way a people cultivates its relationship with nature, with others and with God' (15.5.82). In this sense, culture is never private but shared: it involves the 'common good of each people, the expression of its dignity, freedom and creativity' and a witness of its particular history (*Christifideles laici*, 1988, No. 44).

Quest for truth and love. Different cultures throughout history represent different languages of exploring 'the question of the meaning of personal existence' (*Centesimus annus*, No. 24). But today's intellectual culture suffers from anthropological immanentism, separates ethics from truth, and suffers from widespread relativism (*Veritatis splendor*). The energy hidden in the depth of cultures is love, whereby they 'overcome their incurable finiteness' opening themselves to the mystery of God (22.5.82). Love is also the 'primordial need' of every culture (12.1.90).

Dangers of closedness. Religion is an integral part of genuine culture but today's specialist culture runs the risk of becoming dehumanising. Intellectual culture in particular can close in on itself and remain in 'silence about the transcendent dimension of humanity' or about 'the question of God' (1.11.82). The influence of secular worldviews can damage the range and quality of human questioning which is at the heart of culture: 'A culture without universal values is not an authentic culture' (12.4.87). Or more recently, 'Our time, so rich in technical means, in material means and comforts, often makes do with restricted and relative horizons' (23.9.02).

Church concern for art and creativity. Human self-transcendence expresses itself in privileged ways through 'creative genius' and especially where beauty becomes 'an expression of the absolute' (22.5.82). The very existence of the Pontifical Council for Culture (an initiative of John Paul II in 1982) symbolises the commitment of the Church to the development of culture, and in particular that those involved in creative fields 'may feel that the Church recognizes them as persons devoted to the service of the true, the good and the beautiful' (13.1.89). The Church also counts on them to help people 'rediscover their memory' and 'revive their consciences' (10.1.92).

A privileged space for dialogue. Although, as we will see shortly, with the passage of time more attention has been given to pastoral discernment of the lived cultures of today, contact with intellectual and artistic culture remains a key area for dialogue, especially with non-believers. In this sense culture represents 'a fundamental dimension of the spirit, which places people in a relationship with one another and unites them in what is most truly theirs, namely, their common humanity' (25.3.1993).

Culture as lived

A second and rather different dimension of culture has been increasingly the focus of the Pope's reflections. It is as if he started out in the early years of his papacy with a concentration on the self-conscious culture of artists and thinkers but gradually found himself giving more attention to the lived culture that is such a hidden power in today's world. The spur to deal with this second side of culture was primarily pastoral, as made explicit in a section of the Pope's letter founding the Pontifical Council for Culture in 1982. Having claimed for the second time in the same letter that human destiny is at stake in the field of culture, the text continues:

> Hence the importance for the Church, whose concern it is, of a careful and far-sighted pastoral activity with regard to culture, and in a particular way with regard to what is called living culture, that is, the whole of the principles and values which make up the ethos of a people: 'The synthesis between culture and faith is not just a demand of culture, but also of faith . . . A faith which does not become culture is a faith which has not been fully received, not thoroughly thought through, not fully lived out' (20.3.82).

(That final quotation is from a speech by the Pope of some months

previously.) This passage is significant in various ways: for introducing the theme of pastoral discernment; for its challenging claim
that faith should become culture (the basis for talking about
creating a Christian culture, as will be seen); for its distinction
between culture and living culture.

Discernment of new mentalities

It is notable that in his series of annual addresses to the Pontifical
Council for Culture, John Paul II has increasingly focused on this
pastoral call to understand the lived culture in terms of its humanising or dehumanising influences on people. He spoke of facing
the 'new cultures' of the younger generations, of listening carefully
to the 'latent hopes and aspirations' of people today, and of doing
this with admiration and also 'a clear sense of discernment'
(13.1.83). This task of interpreting the lived cultures has three
characteristics: it seeks to understand local situations and emerging
'mentalities'; its purpose is to prepare and serve evangelisation;
and it would offer a critique of cultural oppression and the presence of an 'anti-culture' (16.1.84). In a period marked by 'profound
changes in mentality' and when 'many cultural milieus remain still
insensitive' to the gospel, the question becomes: 'How is the
message of the Church accessible to the new cultures, to contemporary forms of understanding and of sensitivity?' (15.1.85). 'Basic
to the effectiveness of the new evangelisation is a deep knowledge
of current culture in which the means of social communication
have great influence' (22.1.99).

Even these brief references are proof of a broadening of the
agenda. The mission of the Pontifical Council for Culture was not
simply a matter of contact with the intellectual and creative world
but also of pastoral reflection on the changing sensibilities of people
today. The term 'spiritual discernment' appears with increasing
frequency – to indicate a spiritual sifting of traits of readiness and
sources of closedness for faith. Also much repeated is the link
between 'the inculturation of the Gospel and the evangelization of
cultures' (15.1.86). In this series of addresses the Pope often refers
to inculturation, but never limits it to so-called mission territories;
instead he extends it to all cultural contexts of today. It becomes a

question of discovering the 'language' to reach people in their depths and this is described as 'a cultural and evangelical project of the first importance' (17.1.87). Moreover, such discerning reflection is part of a struggle between a 'cultural void' due to 'the pressures of a culture without spiritual roots' and the hope to 'humanize society and its institutions through the Gospel' (10.1.92). Or nearly ten years later, 'Faith is capable of generating culture . . . culture cannot be reduced to a merely instrumental or utilitarian scope: at its centre is the human being, in all one's dignity and openness to the absolute' (4.10.01).

The possibility of a Christian culture

Although the expression has often been criticised (and is viewed with a certain suspicion within the World Council of Churches, as will be seen), John Paul II has not hesitated to speak of the need for a 'Christian culture'. He put this phrase into the title of the 1992 assembly of Latin American Bishops – 'New Evangelization, Human Development, Christian Culture'. To advocate that faith should become culture means simply that the Gospel can and should permeate 'the ethos of a people, its essential attitudes, its institutions and all its structures'. To counter the absence of 'fundamental Christian values in the culture of modernity', evangelisation today has to 'respond to this crisis of culture' and seek to give birth to 'a cultural alternative that is fully Christian' (12.10.92).

Thus to hope for a Christian culture need not imply a nostalgic regression to some medieval theocracy. Evangelisation of culture means precisely that cultural life – in all its dimensions – can be inspired and transformed by the gospel. However, it must be admitted that the expression 'Christian culture' can give the impression of a return to an old-style uniformity. It needs balancing with a sense of the plurality of cultures, and indeed Fernando Miguens has argued that there can be 'no single Christian culture, but many possible versions of Christian culture; in other words, different cultures can be christianized, yet preserving their pluralism: one should not identify universalization with uniformity'.[9] A recent statement brings together these various concerns, especially the constant stress on culture as a crucial zone of dialogue: 'Attention to culture allows us to go as far as possible in encountering other people. It is thus a privileged mediation between communication and evangelisation' (6.3.02).

Conclusion

Even in this relatively brief summary, it is evident that culture occupies a position of prime importance for John Paul II. During a visit to the University of Riga in Latvia in 1993 he was asked unexpectedly to address a few words in Polish to a group of his co-nationals. He chose to speak – without a text – on culture, and in the course of his improvised remarks offered a quasi-definition of culture as 'all that shapes the human person and the community in which one lives' (13.9.93). This is not the most elaborate or professional definition of culture but it is significant and revealing: it unites the Pope's typical personalism and his sense of community, and although this formulation does not exclude creative or conscious culture, it points more in the direction of lived culture.

As we have seen, Pope Wojtyla was by temperament and training more inclined to the 'higher' culture but his pastoral concern led him to pay attention to the vast field of sociological culture and especially to its trivialising impact. On a visit to the United States he revealed the positive and negative approach together: 'Sometimes witnessing to Christ will mean drawing out of a culture the full meaning of its noblest intentions . . . At other times witnessing to Christ means challenging that culture, especially when the truth about the human person is under assault' (8.10.95). That tendency to raise critical questions about the dominant culture is one which will be shared by the World Council of Churches, as will be seen in the course of the next chapter. It is also a key issue for any discerning spirituality of culture, which will be a principal theme in later chapters here.

Chapter Five

The World Council of Churches: A Different Approach

Culture shapes the human voice that answers the voice of Christ.
(Bangkok Conference 1973)[1]

The gospel is not good news unless it engages the culture of its hearers in a way which takes seriously that culture's identity and integrity.
(Jerusalem Consultation 1995)[2]

The World Council of Churches held its eleventh ecumenical conference on world mission and evangelism in Salvador, Bahia, Brazil in late 1996, with the theme of faith and culture as the main focus for the week. The title was 'Called to One Hope: The Gospel in Diverse Cultures' and a book with the same name appeared in 1998 giving an account of the discussions.[3] This event represented the culmination of a long series of developments within the WCC, a story that has seen the issue of culture emerge from being either ignored or viewed mainly from a missionary perspective; now it is seen as a major theological concern with challenging implications for both the communication and the praxis of faith today.

This chapter offers a brief account of relevant developments within the WCC, mentioning some of the parallels to the Catholic Church's concerns, and also highlighting some significant differences of emphasis. Konrad Raiser, the General Secretary of the Council, has stressed that the current approach to culture is not simply a question of ideas (as in older discussion about Christianity and culture), nor is it primarily missiological. Instead the contemporary focus has returned to basic issues concerning the 'dynamic interaction between the Gospel and human cultures'.[4]

If the core of the gospel is the person of Jesus, Raiser holds that Christian truth is less propositional than an event unfolding in the relationship to God in Jesus Christ. Turning to the companion term 'culture', he insists that its principal meaning now comes from anthropology, thus breaking any easy identification of culture with civilisation or with folklore.

In Raiser's words:

> Culture is the expression of the identity of a human community. Culture refers to the delicate fabric of habits, symbols, artistic representations, tools, rules of behaviour, moral values and institutions through which the human community orders its relationships to nature, to other communities and to reality as a whole. Through processes of socialisation and through tradition, a culture is being transmitted to the following generations. In this sense, culture is specifically human; it is the second 'nature' of human beings in their social relationships. Any understanding of culture includes the language, history, family patterns, etc. of a given community.

This substantial description of culture (reprinted with other texts in the 'anthology' appendix here) gathers together many strands in a way that is partly similar and yet different to that adopted either by Vatican II or by UNESCO. Its highlighting of the 'identity' and of 'community' is stronger than either of those other definitions. By contrast, Vatican II in 1965 (at least in its key paragraph 53) had approached culture largely in terms of a more person-centred humanism. Likewise the UNESCO account (1982) sought to offer a broad synthesis of the range of cultural activities without prioritising. On the other hand this quasi-official WCC definition of 1994 does not mention spiritual or religious horizons explicitly or positively (unlike both Vatican II and UNESCO in this respect); instead it adds a comment that traditional cultures included 'religious symbolizations' while these have been separated from culture in modern societies.

Raiser's article goes on to discuss a tension between 'dialogical' and 'dialectical' understandings of the relationship between gospel and culture. The dialogue model builds on such gospel images as the leaven that penetrates the dough and insists that to be faithful to the incarnation of Christ one has to embrace the human realities of culture rather than judge them from outside.

But the dialectic model reminds Christians of the radical ambiguity of all cultures, of their potential to freeze into destructive and alienating forms, and hence the permanent need for prophetic resistance to any uncritical identification of culture with gospel.

Points of tension and of convergence

Raiser lists three thorny questions that ecumenical discussion encounters in this area.

1.   How can one protect the unique and unchanging gospel in the face of a diversity of *Christian* cultural forms? His solution lies in recognising that there are no timeless expressions of the gospel: the one Christ now has many faces and all faith embodiments are cultural. Tension between the universal gospel and the local particularity is inevitable.

2.   If this is accepted, a fear of relativism arises: are there no criteria for evaluating true and false embodiments of faith? In his view the very question reveals a need for the gospel to become part of a local culture and yet maintain 'critical distance' in order to uncover life-denying aspects of a culture.

3.   Can we speak of a 'Christian culture'? Raiser tends to identity the very idea of a Christian culture with efforts to restore an impossible past in the more complex present.

Some comments by a previous Secretary General, Emilio Castro, offer a crisp summary of insights on culture that have gradually become accepted in this period of WCC reflection.[5]

1.   Culture is not neutral: it can be an idolatrous influence and yet all cultures need to be encountered in a spirit of constructive dialogue.

2.   Cultures are human constructions, and as such bring a mixture of shadows and light. One can add that the WCC uses the term 'discernment' less than in Catholic circles but advocates a similar combination of respect and evangelical judgement.

3.   Culture provides the 'scenario' or 'infrastructure' for the com-

munication of the gospel but it is more than a passive frame of reference: unless evangelisation is reduced to 'soul territory' and forgets about Christian responsibility for the public realm and for all of creation, it includes a task of constant humanisation.

The evolving synthesis within WCC reflection

In 1994 S. Wesley Ariarajah published an excellent pamphlet that summarises the discussion on culture over recent decades. Entitled *Gospel and Culture* it stresses that although the debates have been occasionally repetitive, there is now a significant consensus on the general importance of culture for theology and mission, and also on how to approach some of the key questions involved.[6]

Even before the foundation of the WCC in 1948, the topic of culture was present, if not always explicitly, in many of the deliberations of the series of world mission conferences that started with Edinburgh in 1910. Before the Second World War the tendency was to speak more about the encounter of the gospel with people's religions, and to assume that cultures were simply the outer expressions of different religious systems. 'Pagan' cultures were simply 'in error' and hence converts were expected to renounce both their former religion and culture and take on the 'Christian way of life'. If scant or merely negative attention was paid to culture, this neglect was also in tune with the dialectical theology dominant in those decades: Karl Barth and his followers stressed the discontinuity between the gospel and all human traditions, and they viewed even 'Christianity' with some suspicion – insofar as it can reduce itself to a 'religion' (or what today one might call an 'acculturated' religion).

The post-1945 situation, with all its woundedness, opened new horizons; the challenge of building up nations again brought a new focus on the local churches. Parallel to the process of decolonialisation and the emergence of new nations, a different sense of selfhood was born in the younger churches of Asia and Africa. In the late forties there was much talk about the presentation of the gospel needing to 'adopt' values from people's cultures. Then in the fifties the word 'indigenisation' became popular, meaning not only adaptation of worship but 'relating the gospel to local culture', in the words of the Kuala Lumpur assembly of 1959 (Ariarajah, p. 12). In 1963 the All Africa Conference of Churches came up with the statement that today can seem condescending but was then a courageous step (*ibid.*):

> Traditional African culture is not all bad; neither was everything good. As in all cultures, there were positive factors that held the culture together; there were negative factors which degraded human personality.

Thus a new stage of reflection opened up, which entailed overturning some of the previous theological assumptions within the missionary world. The New Delhi Assembly of the WCC of 1962 (its third general assembly but the first to be held outside the West) confirmed the more generous reading whereby the gospel is not simply disruptive of people's traditions, but can indeed be a force for saving what is deepest in a culture especially in an epoch of crisis and fragmentation. New Delhi suggested a relocation of the tensions involved in this field: instead of the Barthian approach of judgement of culture by the gospel, it diagnosed a more politico-cultural source of conflict in the 'unthinking imposition of Western customs' due in turn to the identification of 'Christian culture' with the West (Ariarajah, p. 25). This assembly, which took place during the same years that the Second Vatican Council was meeting, also attempted a short definition of culture as 'an integrated whole of ideas, traditions, institutions and customs, the setting of the life of a society, usually integrated around a religious faith' (*ibid*).

The Bangkok 1973 missionary conference coined the statement (quoted at the head of this chapter) that 'culture shapes the human voice that answers the voice of Christ', but it also confronted the problem of how the universality of faith need not contradict its particularity. The Nairobi assembly of 1975 went further, viewing plurality as an opportunity for 'exchange between cultures'. In a tone that, as already mentioned, would not find exact parallels in official Catholic discourse, this assembly stated that the question of 'Christian culture' is 'loaded with cultural imperialism'. But it would find echo in Catholic thinking when it went on to affirm that 'no culture is closer to Jesus Christ than any other culture'.

Since commitment to Christ 'takes different cultural forms', the community of the Church is 'called to relate itself to any culture critically, creatively, redemptively' (Ariarajah, p. 33).

Although S. Wesley Ariarajah holds that more recent WCC assemblies and world mission conferences have not gone further on the topic of culture, nevertheless these have been years of consolidating the consensus and of recognising unresolved questions. He himself lists six areas of consensus, which can be paraphrased and expanded as follows (p. 34).

1. The gospel needs to root itself in each culture, finding expression in both life and worship.

2. The previous identification between Western culture and the gospel should be rejected openly, because, in the words of Vancouver (1983), the danger always remains of 'the gospel becoming captive to any culture'.

3. Sensitivity to cultures is crucial in all mission work; otherwise we fall back into attitudes of 'denigrating the receptor cultures' (Vancouver).

4. The gospel does not automatically accept everything in a culture, which is always a mixture of creativity and ambiguity: it also judges, challenges and transforms, and yet the gospel is also 'challenged by the cultures in which it finds itself' to create authentic expressions of Christian life (WCC Central Committee, Johannesburg, January 1994).

5. In an era of such cultural change, one needs to give special attention to the world impact of a secular and technological culture, and how the dominant culture can be intolerant of minority identity.

6. Another ecumenism is needed whereby Christians respect a plurality of cultural expressions of faith among themselves.

With the possible exception of the last point, these key points find practically identical parallels in official Catholic statements of recent decades. Therefore there is a notable convergence of viewpoints, even though there has been little explicit reference to one another.

No 'pure' gospel – no abstract culture

What are the main areas of clarity and of continuing difficulty within the WCC understanding of gospel-and-culture? It has become clearer that theoretical convergences can sound empty unless they are tested in practice. In recent WCC commentaries a lurking idealism has been criticised, one that implies some 'pure gospel' that remains untainted by culture and therefore can be injected, as it were, into the messy field of culture. In theory the transcultural independence of the gospel is widely accepted, but in practice the gospel comes to us in cultural forms. This insight found concise formulation in a booklet of guidelines prepared for local groups: 'The gospel transcends every culture, but it is never accessible apart from its embodiment to specific cultures.'[7]

Especially because of a controversial presentation by a Korean speaker, Professor Chung Hyun-Kyung, at the Canberra assembly of 1991, the issue of 'syncretism' has become a major worry for some members of the WCC. Reluctant to accept her evocation of the Spirit of God in someone like Malcolm X or the suffering rain forests of the Amazon or in goddesses from native religions, Orthodox representatives (and more ordinary orthodox without the capital letter) found themselves wanting to define some 'limits of diversity', a theme that remained a source of tension in the 1996 Brazil conference.

The fine essay by Ariarajah, previously cited, ends by expressing some doubts and disappointments. He notes that some WCC discussions of these issues have been going round in circles, 'taking both an affirmative and cautionary approach to culture' (p. 45). Exactly the same remark could be made of Vatican or Papal statements in these years, even though the assumptions would be different in various respects. As already mentioned, Catholic thinking in this area seems to draw on a more humanist or philosophical sense of culture, and refers to the long history of shared vision within 'Christian culture'. On other issues, the evolution of Catholic discourse on culture in recent times shows many parallels to that of the WCC. There are some significant differences of vocabulary (the Catholic preference to stress 'discernment of culture', as part of 'evangelisation of culture' and 'inculturation of the gospel') but on the whole many guiding insights concerning cultural issues are shared by both Catholics and the World Council of Churches.

Ariarajah traces a fundamental difficulty to the formulation 'gospel *and* culture': this can imply an unhelpful dualism, where the gospel appears 'culture-free' and where a culture is 'devoid of gospel values until in some sense transformed by it' (p. 45). In much the same spirit Christopher Duraisingh has argued that all this discussion concerning culture needs a different 'methodological approach', less deductive and less focused on a 'generic' or abstract notion of culture, and more inductive, grappling with the plurality of cultures. And he links this with the inescapable culturality of the gospel: 'While the gospel is never identical to nor is it exhausted by any particular expression of it, it is not available to us apart from its embodiments in specific cultures.'[8] As noted already, Catholic discussion usually speaks of 'faith and culture' rather than 'gospel', and hence avoids some of these pitfalls, faith having more clearly a human and cultural dimension.

Significance of the 1996 fourfold agenda

As a summary of recent WCC concerns, one can take the four sub-divisions of the 1996 meeting.

1. *'Authentic witness within each culture'*   The key word is 'within' – a point we will find echoed in Catholic discussions of inculturation. In advance of the Salvador conference, the WCC had produced some pamphlets to aid group reflection on these themes and under this first focus some excellent questions such as the following were proposed:[9]

• Where is the gospel comfortable in your culture? Where is it out of place? Do gospel values and cultural values lead you to different actions?

- How do different aspects of your culture enable you to understand the gospel in a fresh way?
- Are there issues in your culture that call for change in order to be faithful to the gospel?
- In what ways has the practice of Christian life become captive to cultural norms?
- Can you identify life-affirming and life-denying aspects within your surrounding culture?

The report of the 1996 meeting for this section highlighted 'discerning the Spirit at work in all cultures', and how this task is always a question of sifting the necessarily ambiguous field of human culture (*COH*, pp. 30–1).[10] It also recognised the many ways in which religion and culture can interact, both constructively and destructively, and it gave priority to a transformation model whereby 'the gospel becomes incarnate in the culture in which it is proclaimed' (*COH*, p. 34).

2. *'Gospel and identity in community'* This dealt with the more 'structural dimensions' of culture and how power relationships can manipulate cultures. It examined how a dominant and global 'mega-culture', with its powerful market and media pressures, can be a destructive and secularising influence, and reflected on how the gospel can be a source of a liberating culture of resistance. Hence this section opened up the issue of secularism and the impact of consumerist lifestyles as promoted by the culture of images and the mass media.

In addition this topic recognised that authentic self-expression by minority or ethnic cultures may be crushed in the name of uniformity; alternatively, narrowly nationalistic claims for identity may be a source of division and even violence against the human community.

Among the discussion questions suggested for this second focus were the following:

- In what ways can Christians acknowledge complicity in the oppression of minority cultures?
- What cultural factors foster situations where the rights of

women are denied or where the poor are excluded from full
participation in the community?

- What is the mission of the Church where communal conflicts
  on the basis of religion are perpetuated?
- In what ways are Christians called to be counter-cultural in the
  face of value systems contrary to the gospel?
- How can Christian congregations be prophetic before such
  transnational forces as the media and market economy?

In fact the report on this section highlighted 'media globalisation',
noting how the image industries promote 'redemption through
consumption', which is not surprising since they are 'driven by
those who control the world market' (*COH*, p. 51).

3. *'Local congregations in pluralistic societies'* This section explored
issues that are important in particular local contexts. It acknowledged the new complexity of culture caused sometimes by the
presence of other religions in a given country or else by plural
identities within individual Christian communities. If the previous
heading touched on the vast international influences at work in
today's world, this focus gave attention to concrete situations,
encouraging a search for a genuinely indigenous faith language.
Again the booklet on 'study process' offered a useful set of questions for discussion, from which the following can be paraphrased:

- How much is the celebration of the liturgy capable of relating
  to the day-to-day life of the community?
- How would you go about a 'rereading' of the gospel in your
  context?
- Are there ways of bringing 'youth culture' into more active
  interaction with the gospel?
- How inclusive is your congregation, in the sense of encouraging the participation of those on the margins of society?
  What can foster a relationship of dialogue with people of different cultures and religious traditions?

The report of discussion under this heading explored the problem
of migration and how many Christian congregations have diffi-

culty in welcoming diversity: the temptation is to withdraw into 'comfort zones for the familiar' (*COH*, p. xii).

4. *'One gospel – diverse cultures'*   This is where the thorny questions of syncretism and of limits to diversity were faced. More positively under this heading the hope was to celebrate some of the cross-cultural richness that is possible when the gospel is genuinely rooted. The report on this section adopted the term 'inculturation' more definitely than in previous WCC documents and in this way came closer to Roman Catholic vocabulary. Although some delegates wanted a gospel 'unaffected by history' which could be translated into different cultural idioms, this was judged to be a merely 'instrumental' approach to culture (*COH*, p. 197).

From a long list of questions for reflection, the following can be selected as indicative of the agenda:

- How can the witness of Christians who belong to another culture challenge, judge and enrich you?
- What are some 'signs of authenticity' whereby contextual expressions of the gospel can be assessed?
- When does a way of evangelism become coercive and lead to proselytism?

The report from this section expressed itself with particular conviction:

> Any authentic understanding of the gospel is both contextual and catholic. The gospel is contextual in that it is inevitably embodied in a particular culture; it is catholic in that it expresses the apostolic faith handed down from generation to generation within the communion of churches. (*COH*, p. 65)

It is obvious that this world conference represented a great step forward in the whole field of reflection on culture from the point of view of Christian faith. In some aspects the issues confronted are remarkably similar to Catholic perceptions; in other ways they raise different issues and approach the whole field from a somewhat different angle. In their reading of the contemporary culture both Catholic and WCC commentators recognise certain key fea-

tures of today's context: a realisation of the omnipresence of culture
– in its many levels – as a shaping but ambiguous influence on
religious faith; the evolution of a global culture that can be the
carrier of a secularist ideology; the struggle for particular cultural
identities as both valid and yet capable of dangerous militancy
today; a sharper awareness of cultural pluralism and of the challenge to incarnate Christian faith in ever-new ways appropriate to
local needs and sensibilities; a new awareness of many peoples as
being in a post-colonial situation and of the 'polycentric reality' so
frequent in today's world.

In short, there is an inescapable doubleness of culture as a source
of possible deception and yet as a stimulus for new languages of
faith. On the one hand people are seldom 'conscious of the cultural
captivity of their understanding of the gospel'; on the other hand,
we have not appreciated enough how cultures positively 'shape
our response to Christ and open the gospel story for us in a fresh
and wondrous variety of ways'.[11] That recognition of culture as
both dangerous to faith and essential for faith is central to any
theological reflection in this field: culture can indeed block the
hearing of the Word but it is also a key zone of human imagination,
capable of fostering new languages of faith worthy of today's
emerging sensibilities.

Chapter Six

Incoming Tides of Modernity

The parameters of our world-view are the presuppositions of a scientific culture. (Jane Collier)[1]

The transformations which ushered in modernity tore the individual from its stable moorings in traditions and structures. (Stuart Hall)[2]

George Eliot begins and ends her greatest novel *Middlemarch* with references to St Teresa of Avila. At first it seems a surprising choice for such a deeply thought-out unbeliever, but she is seeking to evoke how the world of the individual had changed with the arrival of modernity, and not always for the better. Teresa becomes a symbol of existence rooted in a 'rapturous consciousness of life beyond self', where the person is embedded in a tradition of 'coherent social faith' and is therefore free to have an impact on history. But on the final page Eliot meditates, in her eloquent way, how the cultural 'medium' that gave space for contemplative and epic action to Teresa 'is for ever gone'. 'For there is no creature whose inward being is so strong that it is not greatly determined by what lies outside it.' But what lies around us now is the collapse of coherence connected with modernity, so that we are all condemned to 'insignificant lives', filled with the hidden generosity of 'unhistoric acts'. Supportive tradition and community have given way to a new solitude of the unanchored self. This sense of radical loss is one note in the chord of modernity, and yet such loss is not the whole of the story, as these pages will try to explain.

The sentences quoted above as epigraphs are typical expressions of the crisis caused by the arrival of modernity, especially in Europe. Modernity here stands for a cultural condition, as distinct from modernisation which refers to more technical developments such as means of transport or of production. The two went hand in hand but the end result was a greatly altered context for human belonging and human self-understanding, entailing a gradual but total break with pre-modern ways of life. It is a story that has been told many times and in many different tones. Sometimes it is narrated as a drama, hinging on a tension between scientific thinking and an increasingly homeless self (as in those pages of George Eliot). The arrival of modernity has often been linked to one or other event or historical moment; however it is better to think of it as a long incoming tide over centuries. One can identify particular 'waves' but, from the perspective of faith, modernity is a slowly accumulating phenomenon, resulting in a set of assumptions that made religious adherence of an older kind untenable for masses of people.

Since the long pastoral history of Christianity had been formed by pre-modern assumptions, suited to a village or largely rural society, the arrival of modernity posed a major cultural challenge for the Church. The embodiments and roots of faith that had proved sturdy in a simpler culture inevitably became less fruitful and even counter-productive in this emerging cultural situation. Hence it is hardly surprising that church responses remained negative for a long time and that only with the Second Vatican Council did the Catholic Church enter into a more open dialogue and opt for a more positive interpretation of modernity. Some have commented that this reconciliation is a classic example of the Church arriving on the scene in time to embrace what was being severely questioned, just before 'the modernity which the Council seemed to endorse has been converted into postmodernity'.[3] Others have accused the Council of bending over backwards to the extent of offering an excessively rosy portrayal of modernity. The perspectives elaborated by the Council on culture were explored in chapter 3. Religious interpretations of modern culture will be the theme of chapter 7. The issue of postmodernity will then be dealt with in chapter 8. The aim here is to introduce the terms of the debate by offering a sketch of the evolution of modernity and its significance.

Successive waves of modernity

With a certain irony Leszek Kolakowski has remarked that 'how far back modernity may be extended depends, of course, on what we believe constitutes the meaning of the notion'.[4] Indeed many candidates have been presented as claiming to be *the* origin of modernity. But clearly any competition of this kind that expects to produce a sole victor is ill conceived. Modernity is best viewed as a complex phenomenon, a product of converging forces through various centuries.

The long debate about its possible beginnings serves, however, to identify the many ingredients that make the accumulating reality called modernity – at least as regards the Western world. According to Louis Dupré, the origins of this phenomenon can be placed as far back as the nominalist school of philosophy and subsequent intellectual changes between 1400 and 1600. In his view that separation of words from reality became a seedbed for later fragmentations, and thus the complex story of modernity entails a 'spiritual revolution' over several centuries.[5] Once the emerging modern individual feels no longer any embeddedness in the surrounding world, religious anchors decay almost automatically. For Dupré the medieval divorce of the knower from the known opened the door for later claims that self-expression was *the* source of human meaning. This in turn became the cause of a gradual erosion of a religious sense of transcendence. If self is all, who needs society or religion or even culture? In this way alienation comes to be part of the lived assumptions of modernity.

Other commentators suggest more predictable moments from about 1500 on, showing how modernity gradually produced a new culture over about four hundred years. For instance, the Renaissance brought a whole new self-awareness of history, of humanism and of individuality, symbolised by the new dignity of the body in the art of Michelangelo, or by the new drama of individual consciousness in the plays of Shakespeare. Another strong candidate as seedbed of modernity overlaps in time with the Renaissance: the Protestant Reformation is credited by many scholars with being an essential stepping stone in the formation of 'modern' culture, especially through its stress on the relation between the individual conscience and God, independent of mediations such as religious institutions. And of course the spread of the Reformation was deeply linked to a technological breakthrough: it exploited to the full the new era of printing, the so-called Gutenberg Revolution.

From both the Renaissance and the Reformation a new sense of the individual entered Western culture. Some time later come the developments in philosophy associated with Descartes, significant for the parallel phenomena of rationalism and subjectivism. Intimately connected with this rationalism is the Scientific Revolution with its new stress on empirical criteria of truth, and the consequent clash with an unready older culture symbolised in the famous Galileo case. At the same period Francis Bacon proclaimed that knowing was power (*scire est posse*) and Machiavelli laid the foundations of a new politics without moral preoccupations. In this way modernity became a proud form of self-assertion and of human confidence in its own powers, and found itself, almost inevitably, in rebellion against older forms of order and of philosophy.

The significance of this period of early modernity was eloquently captured by Hannah Arendt:

> Three great events stand at the threshold of the modern age and determine its character: the discovery of America and the ensuing exploration of the whole earth; the Reformation, which by expropriating ecclesiastical and monastic possessions started the two-fold process of individual expropriation and the accumulation of social wealth; the invention of the telescope and the development of a new science that considers the nature of the earth from the viewpoint of the universe.[6]

From these precise beginnings modernity went on, in her interpretation, to foster a new self-image of humanity – one rooted in the 'principle of utility',[7] and neglectful of larger horizons of personal action and creative freedom.

Moving forward a century or so, many would see modernity as rooted in the so-called Enlightenment with its insistence on the right to freedom on various levels, freedom of thought, freedom of speech, freedom from religious control, and so on. Thus the emerging rational self took another step towards emancipation from tradition and its various controls. All these inherited ways of life came to seem rooted in unthinking prejudice. Linked with this was the whole political movement most clearly embodied in the American and French Revolutions, which inaugurated different forms of democracy. Enlightenment and Revolution together represent a certain revolt against institutions and against older forms of authority, and because of this both of these developments undoubtedly frightened the nineteenth-century Catholic Church, and caused a response of suspicion and resistance.

Looking more to social rather than intellectual or political history, one has to mention the Industrial Revolution, the arrival of capitalism as a dominant economic system, and the resulting upheaval of urbanisation. Modernisation – as the institutionalisation of new methods of production and related lifestyles – is linked here with modernity as a new cultural consciousness. England was probably the first country in world history to have the majority of its population living in towns and cities of more than about ten thousand people, something that occurred around 1830 or so, largely due to the new technology of the railway. Industrialisation also represented a major crisis for how we live together as human beings, since it brought about a historically new phenomenon known as mass society; as such it is often criticised for its erosion of older forms of community and the introduction of a mass-produced commodity culture. At the same time work patterns change and the new social situation has an enormous impact on traditional rhythms of family life. Clearly, all of these changes constituted a major challenge to traditional and more rural embodiments of religious faith.

The aspects of modernity already mentioned are often interpreted as cultural sources of secularisation, not only in the sense of a diminishing of the external control of the Church on social institutions, but also in the sense of a decline of religious adherence and the retreat of faith into the private realm. In this regard the nineteenth century also witnessed the birth of quasi-universal education and the consolidation of the new secular elites in the intellectual world. Universities became largely non-religious spheres of influence.

The twentieth century brought further developments that complete the complex accumulation that is modernity: electronic communications represent the biggest cultural revolution of recent times, with the arrival of radio, then television, and finally computers and information technology. The very rhythms of human consciousness have been altered by this world of fast-moving data and of images.

The significance of modernity

Even from this skeleton and necessarily simplistic history, some of the multiple strands of modernity come into view, as well as their impact on self-understanding. It altered the cultural conditions of possibility of the 'hearing' from which Christian faith is born: not only did the supportive and cohesive society of pre-modern times fade away, but during these centuries Churches found themselves fighting various rearguard actions on several fronts and facing new challenges to the credibility of faith itself.

According to Louis Dupré, 'modernity is an *event* that has transformed the relation between the cosmos, its transcendent source, and its human interpreter'.[8] This implies that a living synthesis fell apart, and that deep connections between nature, God and human beings underwent drastic change. As early as 1610 the poet John Donne was expressing this sense of crisis in his 'First Anniversary':

> And new philosophy calls all in doubt
> The Element of fire is quite put out . . .
> 'Tis all in pieces, all coherence gone.

But if modernity, for some interpreters, meant loss, for others it meant gain, and in particular the emergence of human self-confidence in a way that was never so conscious in previous cultures. With the arrival of 'modern' culture human beings came to see themselves as capable of experiencing, understanding and being responsible for the world in excitingly new ways.

Three social thinkers: Habermas, Touraine, Taylor

There are whole libraries of philosophical and sociological interpretation of modernity. Here the aim is more modest – to identify some of its principal strands and how they impinge on religious faith. Consulting three of the specialists in the field will help to clarify the main issues.

Jürgen Habermas is famous for his defence of modernity in spite of what he acknowledges as its contradictions and dark sides. He finds it ironical that, with modernity, human beings became capable of shaping their own history and yet its very complexity deprived them of control over it. However, instead of joining those who view modernity as a failure and proclaim the new era of postmodernity, Habermas views it as a historical project that remains incomplete and that is worth continuing. In positive terms modernity 'is essentially characterized by the notion of individual freedom' in science, in self-determination and in self-realisation. He sees these ideas as already part of our assumptions about life: 'They are inserted into everyday communicative practice, and thereby into the life-world.'[9] Certainly modernity was character-ised by the dominance of rational-purposive methods of action, but its crucial contribution lies in the field of human autonomy; for Habermas these two realms need a third area of active com-munication in order to bridge the gap between reason and human values.

In a forceful and recent book Alain Touraine echoes this line of thinking from a different angle; he highlights 'the central cultural issue of the Subject', meaning the free individual who resists the imposed system as a matter of 'cultural choice' and thus becomes a social 'actor'.[10] Touraine's thesis rejects any easy identification of modernity with the forces of rationality alone, insisting that the divorce of reason from the realm of individual freedom underlies the disillusionment over modernity voiced for some generations now. It is as if one twin became dominant and the other retreated into a passive and private realm. Thus we have suffered a painful history of separation between the objective worlds of the economic system, work and technology and the subjective worlds of culture, meaning, freedom and creativity. In Touraine's view the contem-porary dominance of the mass media only deepens this split because it is rooted in a liberal and consumerist ideology and because it seeks to dissolve the Subject's real freedom through the 'rule of commodities' and a 'rejection of transcendence' or the spiritual dimension of life.[11] Until we have some reconciling dialogue between rationality and subjectivity, we are condemned to a double dictatorship – of alienating systems and of narcissistic explorations of consciousness by an ultimately impotent self.

Rather like Habermas' insistence on communicative action, Touraine adds 'community' as a key area along with freedom and rationalisation, and sees this trio as capable of rescuing us from the distortions of a modernity over-identified with reason and system and forgetful that we are 'creatures of desire and memory who belong to a culture'.[12] In this way he proposes to reunify the fragmented field of modernity and to overcome the 'limited' modernity we have so far experienced. Equally he hopes that a rediscovered role for cultural 'actors' can build up a resistance to the 'programmed' society of consumerism and self-interest. Although he is not offering an explicitly religious response to modern culture, he expresses in almost biblical language his urgent hope that the subject-as-actor assume ethical responsibility for the wounded of the world: 'Anyone who claims to be a Subject and ignores his neighbours who are being reduced to silence or death, is deceiving neither himself nor anyone else.'[13]

Touraine, however, is not naive about the conflictual nature of his thesis, and somewhat akin to Samuel Huntington (as mentioned in the Introduction here), he foresees 'conflict between cultures' as more radical now than in the classical era of industrial modernity, especially because of the lack of any community of vision today. But he adds, significantly, that 'cultural traditions are more alive than many people thought'.[14]

A shift in sensibility

Charles Taylor, the Canadian philosopher, has offered some stimulating and positive readings of modernity. Like Touraine he focuses on the centrality of the self, but he views it more in terms of a whole shift in sensibility over centuries and he is also more interested in religious questions. Touraine and Dupré would also agree with him that many influences in modern culture push us towards a dangerous 'subject-centredness' and that 'overcoming it is a major task, both moral and aesthetic, of our time'.[15] Like other commentators on modernity, Taylor discusses the role of disengaged reason and of the self-determining person; but in order to explain the new secularised consciousness, he gives special attention to two other factors: how ordinary family life changed its values with the rise of middle-class culture in the eighteenth century and the different kinds of inwardness and expressiveness that also came to be major values. Since, during the same period, God was often presented as a distant explanation of the natural order, existence came to seem liveable without religious faith. In this way, and for the first time in history, one could cultivate a moral sensibility of benevolence and not necessarily believe in God.

Taylor traces how the self-expression central for Romanticism has narrowed today into the 'human potential movement' and into the 'shallowness' of a culture of subjectivist fulfilment. In this respect the final page of his major work affirms, with disarming simplicity, that 'we tend in our culture to stifle the spirit'.[16] It would be what he calls a 'mutilation' not to retrieve the spiritual aspirations that the complex evolution of the modern self neglected. Where Touraine puts his trust in a renewal of social agency to resist the inherited damage of modernity, Taylor looks more hopefully at the forgotten religious dimension of culture.

In a series of radio talks, this Canadian thinker develops his own discernment of the culture of modernity. He has misgivings about how self-absorbed individuals have lost a sense of any wider participation, or how technology seems to 'flatten' our lives, or how a 'soft' despotism of the state induces powerlessness in its citizens. He also worries about a serious 'loss of freedom' as the shadow side of modernity's great achievements.[17] But he remains a strong defender of those achievements and of the continuing potential of modernity to be redeemed in spite of everything. There is a major struggle going on between the more genuine and more trivial faces of freedom, and hence the key question becomes how to sift out the wheat from the weeds, and how to nourish the wheat of authentic living today.

In Taylor's judgement, there is 'an extraordinary inarticulacy' about the 'constitutive ideals of modern culture', and this silence stems from a 'liberalism of neutrality'.[18] The alternative to this is not an easy and negative judgementalism about 'permissiveness';

rather one needs to inquire into the 'moral force behind notions like self-fulfilment', in order to save what is generous and valid at the heart of modernity.[19] In this respect he proposes two criteria for discernment:

> I want to show that modes that opt for self-fulfilment without regard (a) to the demands of our ties with others or (b) to demands of any kind emanating from something more or other than human desires or aspirations are self-defeating, that they destroy the conditions for realizing authenticity itself.[20]

In other words, cut-off versions of individual freedom, that have little or no social conscience or little or no consciousness of ultimate values, will thereby lack authenticity. It is a quietly powerful argument for renewing the role of the social agent (like Touraine) and renewing the link to religious transcendence (like Dupré). It is also an impressive critique of the 'anthropocentrism' of modernity that can idolise 'choice itself', without reference to further meanings and goals.[21]

The challenge, as Taylor sees it, is to imagine self-responsible forms of life and in this way to rescue the fundamental achievement of modernity. The only way to fight fragmentation, he argues, is to 'strengthen identification with the political community', and towards this end our positive freedoms 'are not zero': 'We are free when we can remake the conditions of our own existence, when we can dominate the things that dominate us.'[22]

A more recent lecture by Charles Taylor, entitled 'A Catholic Modernity?', raises more explicitly religious issues which can serve as a bridge between this chapter and the following one. Arguing that it is dangerous to dream of a total fusion of Christian faith and any particular culture, Taylor sees a more positive Christian valuing of this life as emerging from the tussles with modernity. He acknowledges a Janus-like element in modernity in that it mingles together 'both authentic developments of the Gospel, of an Incarnational mode of life, and also a closing off to God'.[23] This tendency to deny transcendence derives, in his view, more from a new moral self-image in the culture than from any philosophical positions; indeed when it becomes ideologically atheist, it stifles deep human desires and can put valuable gains of modernity in danger. Taylor's hope for believers is that we can gradually 'find our voice from within the achievements of modernity'; in spite of the scandals of church history, past and present, he voices his confidence 'that the love of God is something bigger and more important and more powerful than all this human bumbling and evil'.[24]

In a later section dealing with discernment of culture, more explicitly religious perspectives will be offered for responding to our cultural situation. However it is worth noting that from three such academic thinkers certain principal issues come to the fore that will also prove relevant for our later discussion: the sense of fragmentation, the divorce between social system and personal dimensions, the danger of closed-in individualism, the need for cultural analysis and for an honest facing of conflict areas, the threat of passivity represented by the media world of images, and the importance of community for any healing of the cultural ills of today.

Chapter Seven

Religious Responses to Modernity

> *Modernity is not a world, but the limits of the perspective in which we find ourselves.* (David Walsh)[1]

> *It would be profoundly ironic if, after all the beatings it has received from modernity, religion could somehow unintentionally help modernity save itself.* (José Casanova)[2]

As seen in an earlier chapter, for the Catholic Church the Second Vatican Council represented a moment of conversion from attitudes of rigidity and suspicion before modernity to a remarkably more optimistic reading of contemporary culture. Indeed some of the statements of *Gaudium et Spes* would have been regarded as less than orthodox exactly a century previously, when official church stances seemed to condemn practically all significant developments in thinking and politics. The Syllabus of Errors of 1864 became famous in this respect, with its refusal to reconcile itself 'with progress, with liberalism and with recent civilization'; while such a statement was understandable within the Italian situation of that time, it came to symbolise an extreme of ghetto reaction by the Church against the then modern world. As against this, one can set a 1994 statement of Pope John Paul II which offers a particularly positive evaluation of modernity: 'If by modernity we mean a convergence of conditions that permit a human being to express better his or her own maturity, spiritual, moral and cultural, in dialogue with the Creator and with creation, then the Church of the Council saw itself as the "soul" of modernity.'[3] What is implied here is an embracing of history as an adventure of freedom and a fresh interpretation of modernity as potential ground for Christian growth and authenticity, not simply as a negative challenge or danger to be warned against and avoided. Indeed this way of seeing modernity seems in harmony with that of the sociologist José Casanova cited in the epigraph to this chapter. Casanova studied the response of Catholicism to modernity in countries as different as Poland, Brazil, Spain and the United States, and came to the conclusion that where religion tries to resist the whole 'process of modern differentiation', and in particular the new sense of human autonomy born from the Enlightenment, it will simply fail and suffer 'religious decline'. But when religion discerns and accepts what is genuine within modernity, then not only can it find new authority for itself within the open societies of today, but it can save modernity from some of the 'inhuman logic' of its own unbalanced ideology.[4]

Apart from official church positions, religious responses to modernity in recent decades fall predictably into two main families. Some commentators stress the breakdown of meaning and values, and advocate resistance to the damaging impact of modernity; this interpretation may or may not include a certain nostalgia for a previous unity of culture, but frequently it reads the cultural context as decidedly unfriendly to faith. On the other hand one finds an emphasis on the vast improvement of the human lot brought about by both the new ideas and the new technologies, and also a more positive reading of modern cultural horizons from the point of view of religion and faith.

Perhaps three major principles have guided theological reflection on culture within Catholicism during recent decades. First, culture is seen as a place of human transcendence and hence of creative encounter with God. Second, since all culture is a human construct, it remains a source of ambiguity always in need of discernment and purification. Third, the culture of any particular place or time must play an essential role in the mediation of faith for people in diverse contexts of receptivity for the gospel.[5] Such general lines of approach are clearly of relevance to the whole inculturation debate, but they also underlie the long attempt to forge a religious interpretation of modernity.

In recent years many assumptions about the impact of modernity on religion have been questioned. Does it automatically entail secularisation? Peter Berger holds that Western Europe is the major exception here and that 'the world today is massively religious', as against the 'secularized world that had been predicted (whether joyfully or despondently) by so many analysts of modernity'.[6] In all probability 'desecularised' cultures are going to remain the normal setting for most people on this planet. Moreover, was modernity really a rebellion against Christianity? 'The spiritual background of modernity' was essentially Christian: the roots of 'modern rationality' lay within the long adventure of Christian philosophy.[7] If so, any wise response to modernity would hope to heal the tragic divorce whereby reason shrank to the utilitarian and lost its full range of reaching out to the transcendent. In short, apart from the reinterpretation of modernity in the light of postmodern thinking, some of the supposed opposition between religion and modern culture is now seen as over simple.

Different generations of Catholic interpretation

Christopher Dawson was probably the most distinguished historian of culture working in the period prior to the Second Vatican Council. His constant emphasis was that in all the great civilisations, cultural creativity went hand in hand with religion. Looking at the whole trend of modernity he wondered if one can genuinely speak of a 'culture' if the religious horizon becomes so absent or impotent: if 'detached from spiritual aims and moral values', the living whole that is culture finds itself 'faced with a spiritual conflict of the most acute kind'.[8] As he pondered the 'weakness of Western culture' today, he saw modern education as having 'no sense of revelation'; in a society swamped with 'mass-mindedness', the older symbolic richness associated with cathedrals and worship seemed set aside. Therefore modernity (although Dawson does not use that word) had left people bereft of a 'spiritual sense of religion as an objective reality far transcending one's private experience'.[9] Modernity, in this light, is a case of unbalanced growth, where the mentalities of secularism and technology are incapable of healing the broken unity of a previously spiritual culture.

Among the classics of theological reflection on modernity, pride of place must be given to Romano Guardini's *The End of the Modern World*. Although dating from the late forties, it now seems a forerunner of many commentaries on postmodernity that have appeared within the last decade, and which express themselves with less elegance and much more jargon. In terms similar to those used by Touraine and Taylor forty years later, Guardini diagnosed a loss of an 'objective sense of belonging to existence' at the outset of the 'modern' period, and hence he saw a mixture of existential insecurity and 'the experience of subjectivity' as characterising the new culture.[10] Modernity produced a phenomenon previously unknown to history, the autonomous personality without roots, and this in turn gave rise to a quest for 'culture' – in the sense of creating a human-based world of meanings. The secular values of early modernity often asserted themselves with hostility towards Christianity, so much so that faith went on the defensive and risked being perceived as merely negative in the eyes of history:

> The defenders of Christianity complicated the problem by committing many a blunder in their battle with the new order, blunders which made Christianity seem an enemy of the human spirit.[11]

In Guardini's interpretation, such Christian critiques were largely impotent and ironically the real undermining of modernity came from within itself. The 'optimism about culture' at the roots of modernity was amply disproved by the tragedies of twentieth-century history. Its 'deliberate destructiveness' shocked people into .a new distrust born from seeing through 'the illusions of the modern mind'.[12] Twenty years earlier, in one of his most eloquent texts, *Letters from Lake Como* (composed between 1923 and 1925), Guardini had pondered the death of an older organic culture, due to the rise of the technological and 'mass culture of our day'. In his darker moments he sensed that 'the battle for living culture has been lost', but then with more optimism he began to insist that 'our age is not just an external path that we tread; it is ourselves'.[13] Culture, in his view, can only find renewed hope through the retrieval of 'root virtues of earnestness and gravity, both grounded in truth', 'courage opposed to the looming chaos', and the spiritual art of asceticism to help distinguish 'right from wrong and ends from means'.[14]

Guardini is an excellent example of a Catholic response to the culture of modernity in terms of the scholarship of an older generation – the period prior to the Second Vatican Council. Unlike the

Council he remains reluctant to recognise a wider anthropological meaning for 'culture', and hence he is slow to use that term for anything that does not serve the spiritual unity of society. He is deeply dismayed by the arrival of 'mass culture', interpreting it as inevitably impoverishing. And yet he obviously resists his own pessimism, and deliberately nourishes his hope in human creativity and the capacity to rediscover ways of wisdom in spite of, or possibly because of, the collapse of traditional culture.

In more recent years modernity has been viewed in terms rather of challenge than as a disaster area for religious faith. Hervé Carrier – who was the Secretary of the newly founded Pontifical Council for Culture for its first decade – has listed several sociological characteristics of modernity as constituting a new field for evangel-isation. He singles out the 'individualization of persons' as of particular relevance: as distinct from the pre-modern situation where roles in society were largely assigned to people by their family or situation, modernity fosters a desire for self-autonomy and sets a higher value than ever before on education and personal rights. These positive developments, however, can degenerate into narrow individualism, causing a tragic 'undermining of human communities' and also a crisis in family life.[15] In spite of the obvious fruits of technological progress, in making possible a dif-ferent quality of existence, commentators have noted the contradictions that arise from modernity. In Carrier's words:

> By giving pride of place to efficiency and maximized pro-ductivity, the technical society has fostered a schizophrenic tendency in behaviour. Individuals are forced to play seg-mented and frustrating roles ... Rationality has supplanted reason, the understanding of overall objectives, and the value of personalized reflection. 'Leave your personal life aside' seems to be the message of modern business, government offices, supermarkets, unions, and political parties ... By a strange paradox, the affluent society has brought about a new form of alienation.[16]

If the shaping influences on people's receptivity for faith are so different to pre-modern times, then a certain 'cultural action' by believers becomes imperative: it is not enough to analyse the dominant lifestyles or to describe the problem areas; the future depends on a discernment that can actually 'mould cultural reality'.[17]

Gospel and culture reflections in England

That call for faith to become culture has been paralleled in a whole movement of Christian reflection in Britain in recent times. Bishop Lesslie Newbigin returned to England after nearly forty years as a missionary with the Church of South India, only to find himself viewing the culture of his upbringing with more critical eyes. England seemed to have become pagan in a television-moulded way. That contrast of experiences led him to reflect on the impact of post-Enlightenment Western culture on the rest of the world, as well as on its secularising tendencies within Europe itself. In both those different worlds of his ministry, he found himself faced with a similar challenge: how to communicate the gospel to people whose cultural imagination was shaped by other worldviews. On this basis he criticises the presumption of 'an atomic individualism' and the privatised version of Christianity that dominated various forms of Protestantism. He also describes how missionaries brought dubious Western assumptions to traditional societies. Because of their excessive emphasis on individual conversion, many missionaries were insensitive to the community values already present in non-Western societies and were also unaware of the need to convert cultures and not just individuals.[18] As he came to ponder the gospel–culture encounter his insights come very close to what will later be seen as 'inculturation': 'There can never be a culture-free gospel. Yet the gospel, which is from the beginning to the end embodied in culturally conditioned forms, calls into question all cultures, including the one in which it was originally embodied.'[19]

In different studies Newbigin traces the emergence of current Western cultural assumptions, and how, without it being clearly recognised at the time, they gradually made Christian faith socially marginal, if not actually incredible. While appreciating the great breakthroughs in scientific method since the seventeenth century, he discerns some negative side-effects over how we think of truth and of purpose. The very success of empirical methods of experiment leads to the illusion that this is the only dependable form of truth. Where this assumption is accepted without qualification, the biblical picture of God finds itself in deep trouble. The disappearance of the concept of 'purpose' from science in the early modern period (the generations from Galileo to Newton more or less) created ripples of influence well beyond the sphere of science. Until the arrival of modernity science had always presumed that it was uncovering, in some sense, the meaning of a God-given universe. 'Medieval thought saw divine purpose manifest everywhere in the world of nature,' but the effect of the new science was to replace this explanatory approach with another – a world 'governed not by purpose but by natural laws of cause and effect'.[20]

Without being hostile to science, and noting in fact that more recent developments in physics and cosmology break entirely with the Newtonian model, Newbigin concludes that one cannot have dialogue between the gospel and modern culture without recognising definite areas of contradiction: 'It is obvious that our modern Western world constitutes a plausibility structure within which the biblical account of things is simply unacceptable.'[21] Christian faith makes claims about truth and purpose that cannot be reduced to the psychological or the cultural or to private opinion – the only spheres where modernity is content to allow them to have sway. Without other criteria of truth, central Christian realities such as the resurrection of Jesus appear simply irrational in the light of these dominant ways of thinking.

This approach to questions of gospel and culture, initiated by Lesslie Newbigin and developed by others, unites two principal horizons: how intellectual and social history has created a radically different situation for religious belief and a missiological emphasis on the need for conversion of culture. In the intellectual sphere this analysis stresses the influence of an empiricist philosophy on the plausibility of faith, and in this light it sees modernity as causing a crisis over the credibility of religion. In addition, the lived culture is so greatly impressed by the intellectual respectability of science that it tends to accept unquestioningly the retreat of religious truth to areas of personal taste or autonomous choice. In terms of missiology, Newbigin himself has criticised an apparent hesitation over proclamation of the gospel within the World

Council of Churches. If dialogue means simply a 'sharing of life' and if the 'richness of diversity' becomes a dominant value, what happens to the duty to announce the gospel as truth? In all this he discerns a danger that the Enlightenment version of modernity can tempt even committed Christians into a loss of self-confidence and an 'indifference to truth'.[22] As against this suspected failure of zeal, the call is to give faith a voice in the public world of culture and at the same time to encourage an intelligent analysis of the cultural blockages to Christian truth. One of the principal blockages is precisely the assumption that faith is so individual a matter as not to need any cultural embodiments. If that bias remains unchallenged, the very possibility of believing today can be undermined by the secularity of the culture. Similarly if Christian faith does not become culturally vocal and creative, it may become simply a zone of spiritual comfort for the separate self.

This line of interpretation has given rise to a programme or movement entitled 'Gospel and Culture', whose tendency is to offer a fairly trenchant critique of the Enlightenment tradition in the light of Christian faith. Among characteristic judgements of this approach one can list the following:

- 'The privatization and relativization of religion which has taken place in Western culture over the past three centuries amounts to nothing less than a radical falsification of that [Christian] message.'[23]
- 'The reception of the Christian faith within a country is bound up with the "root paradigms" of that country's culture. If the underlying assumptions are not "Gospel-friendly", the Gospel in that country will not prosper ... It follows that a mission to our culture is needed quite as much as a mission to the individuals who live within that culture.'[24]
- 'The excuse of a "multi-faith society" is used to marginalise all religion ... This has nothing to do with our friends of other faiths, who often value the place of Christianity in public life as symbolising the importance of the spiritual, and everything to do with a radically secularising agenda that wants to relegate religion entirely to the private sphere.'[25]

On another front a group of British theologians decided that the more artistic aspects were being neglected in these more socio-logical analyses: in conjunction with a project entitled 'Theology through the Arts' at the University of Cambridge, they have pro-duced a book of essays arguing that works of imagination 'will play an ever more active role in shaping the way we come to terms with the world'.[26]

Other theological responses to modernity

David Schindler, a Catholic theologian and editor of the quarterly *Communio*, would echo some of those earlier evaluations of the ills of modernity; however, he seeks to offer a specifically theological analysis and to concentrate more on North American culture. According to his argument the underlying ethos of American life links two aspects of modernity: the 'driving impulse to order the world without God' and a machine-like model of human relation-ships, where the person is viewed mainly in terms of control and efficiency.[27] Christians often lament the negative characteristics of culture today, as shown in consumerism, permissiveness, the abuse of power or the manipulation of human life itself; for Schindler such moralising is insufficient. Instead, it becomes crucial to identify 'the deeper logic of self-centricity and externality' that rules people's culturally received visions of reality, and then to identify the fundamental clash between such a liberal and 'mechanistic culture' and the radically different vision of human relationships in the light of Christian faith.[28]

According to this analysis, the prevailing culture in North America fosters a utilitarian sense of the autonomy of the self, which manifests itself in 'arbitrary freedom' and in 'use' and 'domi-nation' of others: 'There is a direct link between a subjectivity (or will) become arbitrary and an objectivity (or reason) become *techne*.'[29] Schindler notes that America's religious heritage usually pictures God in strictly 'monotheistic' and 'masculine' fashion, just as the whole culture tends to see human beings as primarily active and productive.[30] Hence an uncontemplative theology has colluded with an externalist culture and a lop-sided sense of human autonomy. The radical answer has to lie in a different spirituality – more christological, more trinitarian, more Marian – because only in this way, according to Schindler, can the culture rediscover the religious sense whereby life is primarily received from God as gift. The opposing 'logic' at the root of modernity – and of its product, 'liberal democracy' – is one of secularisation. Its principal flaw, from a Christian point of view, lies in the promotion of an isolated self-identity divorced from relationships. The response to this woundedness, Schindler insists, is not to reject 'the achievements of modernity' but rather to question them and to integrate them into a more relational philosophy.[31]

In line with Touraine and Taylor, Schindler sees hope in the possibility of deepening 'the interiority-subjectivity that had been the distinctive achievement of modernity'.[32] In other words, the subjective wing of modernity, with its innovative sense of selfhood, remains not only redeemable but a vital entry point for Christian faith into today's culture. These commentators also highlight the whole zone of social belonging and responsibility as capable of healing the fragmenting forces of modernity. Like Newbigin who spoke of the need to convert culture, Schindler identifies the crucial area of transformation: 'A nature not formed in love will tend (of its inner "logic") to express itself in the mechanistic-instrumental patterns of thought and action.'[33] In spite of all its positive developments, the overall impact of modernity is viewed as anti-Christian in its limiting of our self-images to the realms of the useful and the measurable.

Rowan Williams, now Archbishop of Canterbury, has offered a somewhat different history of the 'erosions of selfhood' in late modernity but one that shares the anxieties already outlined in these last pages. In his book *Lost Icons: Reflections on Cultural Bereavement*, he focuses on how the social cement of older times has collapsed leaving a culture bereft of mutual belonging. 'Human cultures, up to the dawn of modernity' had the blessing of a certain language of common life.[34] Now the self-as-gift has given way to a fragmented system of desires. When the relationship with the past weakens, people do not know how to relate to one another, except in a language of rivalry. Where remorse disappears, their sense of good and evil becomes vague. Where immediacy reigns, there is little sense of life as growth in time: in a world of 'timeless consuming egos' even sexual activity becomes 'separated from promise and acceptance' (pp. 49, 171). When the capacity for story and narrative meaning fades, we lack spaces of trusting conversation that might challenge our egoism. I agree strongly with Rowan Williams' suggestion that in this modern or postmodern situation the 'challenge is to do with imagination' (p. 81); our images of ourselves have shrunk and here lies a key reason why both 'adult choice' (p. 86) and religious faith remain culturally inaccessible for many people.

These sober evaluations of modernity represent a certain school of theology today but there are other voices. Indeed Catholic theologians in this respect are described as falling into two opposing schools. There are those, such as Rahner, Schillebeeckx and Lonergan, who try to continue an Aquinas line of 'correlation' or positive learning from the culture. And there are those, such as de Lubac, von Balthasar and Ratzinger, more influenced by Bonaventure or earlier patristic writings, who stress the differentness of faith from any culture.[35] As will be seen in the chapter on inculturation, this can also be interpreted as a necessary tension between an incarnational and a redemptive focus in theology.

What is significant is that the pendulum has swung in recent years towards more caution about the encounter between faith and modernity – as exemplified in the thinkers from various churches mentioned in these paragraphs. They see the fall-out from the European Enlightenment as responsible for many of the cultural pressures that weaken Christian faith: mechanistic thinking, a self-interested market economy that constricts human aspiration to consumerist needs, overweening scientism, reductive theories of human reason, relativism in education, a retreat of values to the private realm of individual fulfilment, and a portrayal of religion itself as a field of merely subjective choice. At the same time as secular thinkers were unmasking the illusions of modernity, Christian commentators, from their own perspective, were also identifying some of its shadows.

If this tendency to judge modernity severely seems to contrast with the more serene dialogue initiated by the Second Vatican Council, it is partly a question of different decades. Where the sixties sought to concentrate on the permanent human achievements of the modern age – especially in the field of freedom and of human dignity – the eighties were more inclined to stress the damage produced by the same complex phenomenon of modernity. The sixties needed to heal the long-standing and mutual incomprehension between Christianity and modernity, but the eighties, without going back on this recognition of positive developments, became more acutely aware that permanent and dehumanising flaws remained within 'modern' culture. This new Christian critique of the roots of modernity will be of relevance when we come – later in this book – to questions of discerning the spiritual contexts of today and the lived culture that structures daily consciousness. Even if the debate has moved on from modernity to more complex issues of postmodernity, the principal challenges arising from modernity remain with us.

Chapter Eight

The Postmodern Situation – Friend or Foe?

> *The deepest crises experienced by any society are those moments of change when the story becomes inadequate for meeting the survival demands.* (Thomas Berry)[1]

> *Postmodernity can be seen . . . as a* re-enchantment *of the world that modernity tried hard to* disenchant. (Zygmunt Bauman)[2]

Some autobiography to begin with: in the academic year 1986–87 I took sabbatical leave from my post as lecturer in English literature at University College Dublin. On my return I discovered that a mini cultural revolution had taken place, largely through the influence of a provocative new lecturer, deeply immersed in post-modernist approaches. As one of the older professors put it, 'that intellectual terrorist is wreaking havoc'. The students were both confused and excited by this postmodern questioning. In terms of literary criticism many of the old assumptions were being under-mined. For instance, the 'author' was banned as smacking of 'authority'. The writer's biography was bunk. Intention was irrel-evant, as was the historical context of literature. The text had no stable set of meanings; instead it was open to a multiplicity of interpretations and feminist readings were particularly in vogue. Word play and exotically surprising echoes between texts were equally cultivated. The old canon of masterpieces of literature was interrogated and found guilty of class and gender bias and the contagion of power. Indeed one could study with equal fruit James Joyce and a column in today's newspaper. If the received literary culture had certain established values and priorities, these were being jettisoned with a certain glee.

Such was my introduction to the challenge of postmodernism. At first I found it both incomprehensible and incredible, but gradu-ally I began to see the point of its radical attitudes and to realise that I had been trained in a particular school of humanistic 'new criticism' that needed to be questioned and qualified. I have added this paragraph not only to incarnate the typical shock of post-modern thinking but to indicate that it has touched practically all spheres of study or research. In particular it continues to have an enormous influence, even dominance, in the human sciences such as sociology, and in humanistic fields like literature and philo-sophy. With this background hopefully we can better understand its multiple impact in today's culture both 'high' and 'ordinary'. Undoubtedly it is a vital influence in contemporary life as the papal encyclical *Fides et Ratio* acknowledged in 1998: 'Judgement on what is called post-modern is sometimes positive and sometimes negative . . . One thing however is certain: the currents of thought which claim to be postmodern merit appropriate attention' (No. 91). This chapter will argue that the postmodern is not only a current of thought but a lived condition of culture today, and indeed that this latter aspect is of particular relevance for religion and theology.

What then are we to make of 'postmodernity'? From the outset, it is important to stress that it is not the same as 'postmodernism'. Even though not all users of these terms give them the same meaning, there is a helpful tendency to use 'postmodernism' for the more intellectual school of thinking associated with Lyotard or Derrida, or even tracing its origins as far back as Nietzsche, and then to reserve 'postmodernity' for a wider cultural context that includes ways of life as well as forms of thinking, and which can be viewed more as a 'sensibility', or as 'postmodernity of the street'. The two realities are not completely separable. Both share a certain questioning of the achievements of modernity but whereas postmodernism seems to remain largely in a mode of refutation, cultural postmodernity, as will be seen, goes beyond negative cri-tique and, in some instances, represents a search for liveable languages beyond the narrowness of modernity. In short, there is a 'deconstructive' or even destructive element in the philosophies of postmodernism, whereas postmodernity can be described as having two wings, one of existential lostness and one of 'recon-structive' exploration of new frontiers.[3]

Although some initial space here needs to be given to 'postmodernism', more attention will be given to 'postmodernity'. Our focus throughout this book is more on lived culture than on thought culture, and hence the emphasis of this chapter will be on the emerging lifestyles and set of assumptions in the globalised situations of today. There exist many theologians who have taken the philosophical wing of the postmodern as a dialogue partner.[4] Since the main postmodernist tendencies in the intellectual sphere seem more vehemently negative than positive, one can summarise them as a set of ten commandments, commenting on how they overturn the typical positions of 'modern' thought. Such a simplified (and even tongue-in-cheek) scheme is offered, not with any intention of completeness, but to indicate in brief some of the radical rejections involved.

The ten commandments of radical postmodernism

1. *Thou shalt not worship reason.* Where modernity, from the excitement of new sciences, elevated instrumental or empirical reason to total prominence, and where Descartes advocated method, certainty and clear ideas, postmodernism becomes disenchanted with such overweening rationalism, and prefers what Vattimo has termed 'weak thought' – with its shyness about all truth claims. Similarly, according to the 'deconstruction' proposed by Jacques Derrida, all reality is like a text, open to a myriad of conflicting interpretations. Instead of the 'modern' assumption that objectively correct answers are possible, we are all caught in a 'prison house of language', where relativism replaces any rationally ordered world. Everything is under construction and nothing is simply 'true'. Meaning, if it exists at all, is created by us and is always in flux, and hence unattainable or, in Derrida's pun, always different and differed. Science itself has abandoned the quest for verifiable certitudes and has become anti-representational, indeterminate and tentative. In various spheres of thought, the 'modern' paradigm of rationality is being unmasked as an emperor with no clothes.

2. *Thou shalt not believe in history.* With a philosopher such as Hegel history takes over from 'nature' as the key category for

understanding existence. Hence where modernity promoted a proud confidence that human beings could at last take history into their own hands, shaping it in line with various aims or visions, postmodernism speaks of the 'end of history', questioning all such large hopes, preferring to live without big goals, content with utility, communicability and an immediacy where there is no real past or future. Where history was considered as a coherent development, implying an order or direction progressing towards some secular salvation, now models of determinacy give way to chance and indeterminacy.

3. *Thou shalt not hope in progress.* Although modernity distrusted absolutes and authorities, it put trust in utopias of progress – what Francis Bacon has called the *regnum hominis* with its evolutionary hopes of overcoming evils and creating situations of happiness. Postmodernism is partly born of the disasters of the twentieth century, most notably the Holocaust, and abandons all such hopes as arrogant and dangerous. Instead it cultivates only the partial and the fragmentary.

4. *Thou shalt not tell meta-stories.* In a similar way modernity lived out various mythic stories of human heroism, such as Prometheus stealing the fire of the gods; but postmodernism rejects 'meta-narratives' as 'logocentric', that is to say, deceived by the inevitable human urge to find one central meaning for existence and to express this meaning in some story form. In so far as Christian faith *seems* an example of a 'meta-narrative', it comes under critique from postmodernism as 'totalising': claiming that it can encompass everything and offer meaning for everything. In short, total explanations are banished (but is genuine religion ever such a closed explanation?).

5. *Thou shalt not focus on the self.* Where modernity from the Renaissance to the Enlightenment gave birth to a new humanism, an exaltation of human beings at the centre of the universe, and stressed psychological identity or the self-contained individual as the measure of all things, postmodernism proposes the 'death of man', in the sense of a radical scepticism about subjective approaches and about the importance given to personality and

self-consciousness in Western culture. The Cartesian notion of a
sovereign rational subject is looked on as an infant's illusion of
omnipotence. In Richard Rorty's view, the self has no longer any
centre or foothold. Others, from an ecological perspective, would
stress that the anthropocentric humanism of modernity made 'man'
into a cruel despot over the cosmos, with a particular insensitivity
to the earth itself.

6. *Thou shalt not agonise about values.* Where modern philosophy
– as in the case of Kant – put questions of morality and freedom
in the foreground of thinking, and where lived modernity tended
to be austere and even puritan in its style, postmodernism cultivates the spirit of both Dionysus and Narcissus: a spontaneous
hedonism goes hand in hand with aesthetic expressions of
autonomy. In this privatised age of immediacy and of images,
moral responsibility is viewed as an illusion inherited from a different era. In its extreme form, life is valueless, moral absolutes
are illusory, and freedom is only a game. No stable points of
reference remain. Their place has been take by a hard-nosed prag-
matism accompanied by a neo-pagan hedonism. The consumerist
model dominates all choices.

7. *Thou shalt not trust institutions.* Where the long process of
modernity saw the evolution of the modern democratic state and
an increasing role for politics in society, postmodernism distrusts
all institutions as manipulative forms of oppression by the
powerful. Michel Foucault proposed that methods of punishment
and imprisonment provide a fitting metaphor of the hidden
tyranny of dominant cultures. Traditions are merely modes of
ideology and control. Churches are inevitably perceived as being
part of the naive and authoritarian past. The culture of obedience
is dead: dance merrily on its grave.

8. *That shalt not bother about God.* From the religious point of
view, modernity gradually made atheism into a plausible philosophy, and for the first time in world history, this rejection of faith
by intellectuals became a widespread stance among the Western
educated classes. Postmodernism does not so much reject atheism
as assume it, outgrowing its militancy about the 'death of God',

and preferring a dismissiveness about the very question of transcendence. The tone has changed radically from argument and confrontation over religion to a vague acknowledgement that occasionally we have 'immortal longings' as Shakespeare's Cleopatra would put it. Immanence comes to be common sense and the need for religious searching disappears. If one must, one can speak of the divine, in the sense of transitory feelings of ecstasy. But beware of the illusory notion of 'presence': absence is all. Hence no transforming word of revelation can speak to us.

9. *Thou shalt not live for productivity alone.* Sociological modernity involved an urbanised organisation of life imposed by the Industrial Revolution. Against the priority given to systems of economic efficiency, a mechanical exploitation of people and of the earth, and the dominant logic of the left-hand brain, postmodernism protests in the name of randomness, aesthetic play, and a range of liberations associated with the right-hand brain. Work is replaced by shopping and the fetish of style. In England, for instance, it is now estimated that more people work in ethnic restaurants than in all the old industries put together – coal, steel, clothes etc. The 'post-industrial' culture is simply a fact.

10. *Thou shalt not seek uniformity.* Culturally modernity was a relentless leveller, imposing a Western-style sameness, believing in universal or typical features of human behaviour, and being blind or insensitive to local traditions. Postmodernism has rediscovered 'difference' as a key value and relishes in the seeming anarchy of cultural diversity. In a very real sense, although postmodern thought was born in the First World, it symbolises a new recognition of other cultures, religions and ways of life. Indeed this more positive aspect is being seen as signalling a decline of the West and hence is lived with enthusiasm in some non-Western societies and at times in Islamic cultures (which seek to avoid the negatives of modernity and to unite tradition with the postmodern).

Apart from the final two responses listed, postmodernism in this presentation appears more destructive than constructive. Its critique tends to ignore the permanent achievements of modernity:

the progress in quality of life due to scientific, technological and medical developments, the deeper sense of human dignity associated with modern democracy and with historical consciousness, the many freedoms offered by changed social situations, the goals of emancipation and equality, the goal of universal education, the autonomy and rights of the individual as against the system – to mention some chief points of breakthrough. Hence 'postmodernism' risks throwing out baby with bath water, through not recognising the enduring contributions to culture from the various 'modern' revolutions. 'Progress' was not simply an empty slogan of the Enlightenment.

As touched upon at the outset, this theoretical 'postmodernism' seems less relevant to questions of faith than 'postmodernity' as a cultural mood or state of mind of recent times. Where postmodernism tends to express itself in a series of nihilist doubts about 'modern' claims, cultural or lived postmodernity, as already mentioned, will be seen to have two streams, one dehumanising and the other opening out to new horizons. This latter involves an important attempt to purify the modern inheritance. It does not play down the shadow sides nor does it reject the great achievements; rather it seeks to discern the tone of our culture, allowing for the excesses and imbalances of modernity, but seeking a healing of wounds rather than a rejection of the whole legacy.

Postmodernity as a cultural sensibility

As suggested earlier, it is helpful to make a distinction between 'postmodernism' as an intellectual reaction against the excesses of 'modern' claims, and 'postmodernity' as a potentially more positive cultural mood of today. For some authors postmodernity entails a radical departure from modernity, but others prefer to speak of 'late modernity', thus stressing that we are in a more advanced and problematic stage of much the same historical process. Anthony Giddens, the Cambridge sociologist, argues that it is premature to label our age postmodern. He prefers to speak of 'high modernity' (or 'radicalised modernity') because 'the consequences of modernity are becoming more radicalised and universalised than before'.[5] Interestingly he sees the zone of interpersonal trust and self-disclosure as forced into prominence because of the lack of anchors in contemporary culture.

Indeed this highlighting of the personal was confirmed during a course I taught at the Gregorian University in Rome. I asked the students to pool their insights on the characteristics of modernity and postmodernity. I filled the board with the answers. They came up with all the stock descriptions of modernity, which fell into two families – one dealing with ideas and ideologies, and another focusing more on the individual self. Thus among the more theoretical characteristics of modernity, we listed: new trust in rationality, in science, in progress, in human control over nature and history, and a parallel distrust of tradition and authority, leading to a spirit of revolution in politics and in the religious sphere the emergence of privatised faith and ultimately of 'modern' atheism. In the other zone of the self, modernity seemed marked by a primacy of individual dignity, personal rights and autonomy of conscience, and therefore by a new sense of self-creative freedom in many fields.

An interesting trend emerged when we turned our attention to the characteristics of postmodernity. A whole series of question marks were placed against some achievements of modernity, as contradictions long present in the modern enterprise came more sharply into focus. Did not the exciting novelties of science become frozen into a dehumanising of truth? Or the arrival of democracy sink into an anchorless liberalism? And so on. But then it became more than a matter of question marks. Instead of having to write down new words on the board, all I had to do was draw a large X over various features of modernity. We ended up cancelling out most of the non-personalist aspects of modernity. Thus, postmodernity looks with deep suspicion at an arrogant sense of reason, at scientism, or naive claims to progress, or insensitive dominance of the earth, or utopias about history. However, we did not put an X over the various forms of subjectivity fostered by modernity (nor over the related theme of rejection of authority). Instead, we discussed how in postmodernity the fate of the self deepens into a new isolation and loss of connections. And yet one of the surprises of postmodernity seems to stem from this loneliness and shows itself in an openness to spiritual searching. On the religious front, postmodernity, at least in some of its tendencies, is less sure or dogmatic about atheism.

In short, the big claims of modernity have fallen under suspicion and come to be largely rejected, but the 'turn to the subject' born with modernity has not only survived the transition but become an even more crucial strand of our lived culture. It has given rise to a new sensibility that can be read either positively or negatively. According to one judgement we have fallen further into isolation, fragmentation and narcissism, where life is an indifferent game and individual options are merely aesthetic and provisional. But according to another reading, the oft-maligned sense of self can be the source of our hope, because permanent hungers of the heart come to expression with new honesty and the quest for liberation and authenticity takes on a new humility. Even the sense of dispersal, according to this interpretation, rebounds into a new spiritual search for community and roots. Spirituality becomes not just a fashionable term but a real issue in this era beyond its being censored or marginalised by modernity.

Modernity, we have seen, caused a fragmentation of three horizons: the sense of self, the sense of truth, the sense of God. The self became lonely, self-conscious and withdrawn (and in literature the novel is born to mirror a new social class and replace the more public genre of drama). Truth, measured mainly with the instruments of empirical science, also withdrew into the sphere of the verifiable. God, as imagined by the defenders of faith in the seventeenth century and later, retreated to theism and even deism: theologians become narrowly rational, forgetful of Christ, and leaving the field of spirituality to sentiment.[6] Even in that same period there was a resistance movement against the ravages of modernity: the pre-Romantic valuing of sensibility gave new depth and dignity to the lonely self, and Romanticism itself sought to save humanity from mere reason and the anonymous city – locating salvation within the world of imagination and feeling.[7]

Two poles of postmodernity

If all these forces were at work in modernity, not just as an ideology, but as an emerging sensibility, in a similar way we can identify two poles within postmodernity. Although the theoretical exponents of postmodernism voice scorn for humanism and the myth of the self, postmodernity has its more hopeful purifiers. Instead of delighting to dance on the grave of modernity, these want to rescue it from its excesses and contradictions. From the point of view of religious faith, these less extreme postmoderns are potential dialogue partners for theology in its reflections on culture and faith. However, as will be seen, there are more paralysed and spiritually empty forms of lived postmodernity, where alienated and consumerist attitudes dominate and the ego drifts without anchors.

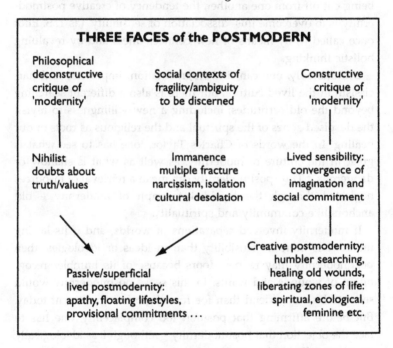

THREE FACES of the POSTMODERN

Philosophical deconstructive critique of 'modernity'	Social contexts of fragility/ambiguity to be discerned	Constructive critique of 'modernity'
Nihilist doubts about truth/values	Immanence multiple fracture narcissism, isolation cultural desolation	Lived sensibility: convergence of imagination and social commitment
Passive/superficial lived postmodernity: apathy, floating lifestyles, provisional commitments ...		Creative postmodernity: humbler searching, healing old wounds, liberating zones of life: spiritual, ecological, feminine etc.

The accompanying diagram tries to capture something of the polarities between theoretical and negative postmodernism (on the left) and an emerging sensibility of postmodernity (on the right). If the left line starts as radical doubt, the right line represents a certain search for new hope. In between, there is the more ambiguous and religiously problematic face of postmodernity: the bored indifference that seems related both to the fragmentation of everyday culture and to the more nihilist theorists. This version of lived postmodernity I call 'passive' or 'superficial' to distinguish it from the 'creative postmodernity' that, as will be seen, offers much more opportunity for dialogue with faith.

Creative postmodernity, in this way, is a new sensibility that aims at wholeness. It sees modernity as having caused an abyss between the rational and the subjective aspects of humanity – by developing both dimensions in isolation from one another. Post-modernity as sensibility is groping towards forms of life that bridge these divisions. Thus where both reason and feeling suffered by being cut off from one another, the tendency of creative postmod-ernity is to overcome this 'dissociation of sensibility' (as T. S. Eliot once called it) by means of new connectedness and by revaluing holistic thinking.

Undoubtedly, one can find fragmentation, impotence and nar-cissism in the lived culture, but there is also a different searching beyond the old certitudes, including a new willingness to revisit the despised zones of the spiritual and the religious as roots of our healing. In the words of Charles Taylor, 'one has to see what is great in the culture of modernity, as well as what is shallow or dangerous'.[8] Thus postmodernity can mean a retrieval of resources neglected through the lopsided triumph of modernity – old anchors like community and spirituality.

If modernity involved separations of worlds, and if its lasting impact lies more in sensibility than in ideas or ideologies, then postmodernity may reopen doors because of its humbler recog-nition of wounds and wants. In this sense postmodernity would seem to be more friend than foe for religious commitment today. But before affirming that position too complacently, one has to face the objection that postmodernity – although less ideologically hostile to religion than modernity – is in fact more apathetic in its stance before possible religious faith.

Most commentators would agree that the postmodern self suffers from a new isolation. The old supports of a cohesive society have almost disappeared. The anchors in religious belonging have less-ened drastically for many people. We live in the wake of multiple fracture, where the individual's various languages of searching are themselves cut off from one another. If this is so, then postmodernity – even in its lived or everyday forms – suffers from an incapacity for roots. This shows itself in the decline of social commitments concerning justice. It also shows itself in a diminished sense of the past, a kind of cultural amnesia. If this is valid, then judgemental 'isms' are unworthy: it is not just a question of narcissism, hedonism, nihilism, post-materialism and so on. It is a question of suffering sensibility, of lostness, of a handicapped quest within a culture that offers few connections with others or with history.

This picture seems at first to be a cultural desert. If faith, ever since we emerged from the easy inheritances of pre-modernity, has had to be a decision against the tide (as in the early centuries of Christianity), then this landscape seems even more a formula for paralysis. Because of little cultural support and little attractiveness in the mediations of religion, faith options become harder to reach, and when one adds in the pressures of trivial postmodernity, the faith dimension can often fade into utter unreality.

But everyone seems agreed, paradoxically, that a spiritual hunger is stronger than in modernity, more acutely so because of the new cultural desolation. The spiritual hunger is real, but with so much religious rootlessness there is a danger of ending up with a floating spirituality very far from the definiteness of Christian faith and one which can even be a form of postmodern unbelief. In spite of this ambivalence, there is a significantly new tone of religious openness. The theologian David Tracy has been concerning himself in recent years with the issue of postmodernity, stressing that it represents both a cultural and a theological category. He views postmodernity as a new sensibility, more open to religious horizons than during the long reign of modernity. He praises the key achievements of modernity – the philosophical maturity born from the crisis of the scientific revolution, the 'bracing honesty of an historical consciousness' the liberating aspects of the democratic ideal – and yet he discerns a dangerous levelling and pride within modernity, a 'drive to sameness, the modern Western scientific, technological, democratic culture that is culture and history', the arrogance of modern liberalism that never says out loud but implies that 'Western culture is culture'.[9]

According to Tracy, it becomes possible to stress again the crucial frontiers between theology and spirituality. Modernity tended to reduce everything to external 'religion' or even to deism. Postmodernity is more open to the religious sense and especially the prophetic, the cosmological and the mystical or participative dimensions of religious experience. A postmodern spirituality will retrieve the wise shyness of a negative theology, reticent to explain its mystery and suspicious of cheap words. A more searching postmodernity calls for a convergence between a sense of God as hidden (but revealed) and God as incomprehensible (but incarnate).[10] Just as the emerging postmodern sensibility has retrieved the value of emotion and affectivity, the religious experience of being-in-love with God has received serious attention in theology.[11]

Towards a balance sheet

Perhaps there is a tendency to be too hard on modernity and too rosy about the more holistic sensitivity of postmodernity. Be that as it may, the case for a positive view of this new cultural mood is based on its double claim – to heal some of the wounds of modernity and to reopen neglected wavelengths of exploration. Where modernity left 'man' lonely and without purpose, postmodernity seeks to expand the set of relationships, cosmic and communitarian, and to reopen the conversation about the ultimate goals of life.

According to these more favourable interpretations postmodernity is characterised by new sensitivities on three fronts: ecology, feminism and the return of spirituality. Indeed the three areas are deeply connected: they are rooted in a realisation that our history has suppressed something precious, which now needs liberation. Modernity was exploitative of the earth and of peoples, forgetful of women and of the feminine in each person, and forced the spiritual dimension of life to retreat to the poetic and the private. If so, postmodernity proposes a series of openings. Already these three horizons, that were not so strongly felt even a generation ago, together represent a major shift in sensibility. In Thomas Berry's expression, our inherited 'cultural coding' remains an impoverished guide in this new landscape: we need to re-imagine our presence to the earth, to the spirit, to the capacity to dream, to our many alienated relationships.[12]

Some Spanish-language theologians seem to offer the most positive readings of this new sensibility, singling out several zones of purification and hope for faith:[13] the return of attention to religious experience, an area despised as illusory by modernity; a healthy distance between religion and manipulative or totalising power systems, as fostered especially by liberation theologies; prophetic critique of the idols of theism (a first cousin of modernity) and of rationally packaged versions of God; a quest for more adequate wavelengths before divine mystery, shown in retrievals of negative theology or narrative theology; renewal in the aesthetic or festive or contemplative aspects of faith (even von Balthasar can be seen as postmodern in a certain sense); a Christianity that faces the challenge of differentness of cultures, overcoming modernity's suppression of this diversity; and while there are new risks of a narcissistic and 'light' religiousness within trivial postmodernity, there is the opposite tendency to trust the limited or fragmentary, and forge a more patient spirituality of option for the poor. Llano speaks of postmodernity as returning to an analogical way of thinking as a non-rationalist and gradualist approach to meaning, and in this he sees hope for linking *praxis* and *poiesis*, which had been long polarised in classical modernity. One finds something of the same 'friendly' diagnosis in Elizabeth Johnson who sees 'postmodern consciousness' as aware of 'the fragility of the human project' and yet prizing 'essential connectedness' and the 'importance of community'.[14] According to Elaine Graham, contemporary feminists have become acutely aware of the gender bias present in modernity; she hopes that postmodern theologies can ground themselves in 'performative' practices of faith communities and in the process of transcendence disclosed in 'the encounter with the Other'.[15]

George Steiner, in his well-known book *Real Presences*, has little patience with an ideological postmodernism for which God is just a 'phantom of grammar'. Such dismissiveness, in his view, is simply 'tone-deaf': if we neglect music, imagination and the arts, 'without which human life might indeed not be viable', we suppress or forget our capacity for wonder, for transcendence and for possible

religious vision.[16] On the other hand, it can be argued, beyond the
old cages of modernity and of closed postmodernism, a 'remarkable opening of the soul is taking place'; writers like Dostoevsky
or Solzhenitsyn, who learned wisdom in the crucible of suffering,
are postmodern in a prophetic way. They point imaginatively to
'the God who for so long has been displaced' from the centre
of culture.[17] In this light postmodernity becomes a movement of
resistance to a long and misguided oppression of the spirit.

Hopes for creative postmodernity

Do we need yet another distinction, perhaps, between passive and
creative postmodernity (as indicated at the bottom of the diagram)?
Passive would point to the drifting nature of contemporary lifestyles – what can be described as the 'alienated immediacy' of
consumerist existence, or as the cultivated cynicism that reigns
in sophisticated circles (echoing the more conscious negativity of
postmodernism). Whereas this passive postmodernity seems in
continuity with the voids of modernity, and religiously is a form
of apathy and distance from the hungers of faith, critical postmodernity questions all that long amnesia. It seeks to forge a new
language of living for today. It reopens doors locked or at least
neglected by modernity. It insists that there is more to life than the
rational system or the dominance of technology. It hopes to find
ways of healing our inherited forms of loneliness – all those separations of self from society, or reason from feeling, or science from
religion, or man from woman, or theology from spirituality, or
individual depth from embracing the struggles of history. Its tone
is one of shy searching, of a healthy suspicion of systems and of
easy certitudes. It is impressed more by praxis than by grand
theorising.

Put like this, it could seem another utopian agenda, doomed to
disappointment. But there is a certain saving humility at the heart
of this postmodernity that starts small, goes one step at a time, and
values the limited horizon of the possible. With this qualification,
disappointments can perhaps be avoided: at its best it seeks to
discern our needed liberations if we are not to suffer from new
oppressions of our humanity and our imagination. This face of

postmodernity – as distinct from the superficial styles or the nihilist militancy – can be a way of reclaiming a space for mystery after the waste lands of secular modernity.

Besides, we need a postmodernity of our own Christian making. It is not a question of watching the signs of the times, hoping passively for a change in the weather, but rather of seeing that already this humbler moment after modernity is itself a friendly moment for creative communication of the Christian vision. Possibilities open up for probing a more genuine sense of self after identifying the damage of false individuality as proposed by militant modernity. Parallel possibilities open up to link this new search of the self with communitarian and spiritual horizons, in ways that have not been culturally credible for centuries.

Perhaps our earlier distinction – between a radical postmodernism of the philosophers and an existential postmodernity in the lived culture – needs qualifying. We have portrayed the latter as dividing into two streams, one dominated by loss and drifting, and the other showing signs of a fresh search beyond the confines of modernity. What seems to be emerging in recent years is a less destructive note in the theorists that links up excitingly with the more creative tendencies of the new sensibility in practice. When a deconstructive thinker such as Jacques Derrida begins (in the nineties) to write books about giving and gratitude, about friendship, forgiveness and new religiousness, something important has changed. Even more significant is the retrieval of the human importance of gift in such writers as the Quebec sociologist Jacques Godbout, who speaks of a relational anthropology symbolised in human giving as taking us beyond the 'modern' paradigms of the utilitarian individual as driven by market-style competition. This now seems a cynical and reductive interpretation of who we are. Instead a capacity for generous gratuity, even to the point of self-sacrifice, is much more fundamental in human beings and in their culture.[18] The giving of gifts, far from being a form of manipulative exchange, is a deep language of human connection. In this sense Godbout's writings are postmodern in a surprisingly positive sense: he gives historical and intellectual backing to the quest for alternative images of who we are. These new tones in the intellectual world also find parallels in more pastoral fields. In Mark

Driscoll's words, 'the modern church is stuck on nostalgia' insofar as it thinks it has to answer the old 'modern' agenda of 'rationalism, empiricism, consumerism and individualism'. In his view teachers and evangelisers, especially of youth, do not yet realise fully 'the postmoderns don't accept modernity's foundational principles'.[19]

When the self is less lonely, when the culture finds its shared language of community on local and world levels of justice, when theology finds common ground with spirituality, then we are talking about a new sensibility that is far from a passing fashion and one that is also being recognised by leaders of postmodern thought. It is a significant convergence of hungers and of potentials in need of discernment and inculturation – topics that are to be explored in subsequent chapters here.

Chapter Nine

Debates about Inculturation

Faith is lived, clothed, enveloped, expressed in a culture.

(Yves Congar)[1]

To think that Christianity will not change a situation is to rob the Christian message of its most important part. (Robert Schreiter)[2]

Inculturation is a recent term for an outreach of faith that has ancient roots in Christian history.[3] It is also a battleground between various schools of thought over faith and culture. To put it simply, there is a theology of the desk, as often found in official church documents, and a theology of the field, produced by those directly involved in seeking to inculturate the faith. The former tends to evoke large hopes of mutual enrichment, couched in general and usually cautious language. The latter starts from the local situation and soon runs into tensions and delicate issues of discernment. From the perspective of the desk or the library, inculturation can seem a smooth and gradual process 'from above'. But out there in the field of society and praxis, things become more complex and conflictual. There is a danger that some discourse about inculturation, written without living interaction with particular cultures, can remain in the mould of what Newman would call 'notional' rather than 'real'. At the end of this chapter we will explore these differences of perspective. By way of introduction, however, let us recall how the Christian faith was faced with cultural pluralism from the very beginning of its history.

The very fact that Christians have four gospels and not one is a powerful symbol of how preaching the good news was shaped from the beginning by the needs of different audiences with their different assumptions. Thus the Gospel of Matthew is aimed mainly at people of Jewish background (with its many quotations from the Hebrew scriptures) whereas the Gospel of Luke concerns itself more with the religious questions of those from a Hellenistic culture (and according to the experts is expressed in a more flowing and literary style than the other synoptic gospels). Again the simple but surprising fact that the New Testament is written and comes down to us in Greek, and not in the language of Jesus himself, is another indication of a crucial decision by the early Christians – to communicate creatively beyond Jewish circles to the culture of the Gentiles. Indeed that pastoral option tore the early Church apart and nearly caused a split in its ranks, as is seen from the tense debates reported in Jerusalem in Acts 15. These inter-cultural encounters also provoked strong emotions within people. St Paul (as will be seen in more detail in the next section) underwent a significant conversion of attitude in Athens, and took a sympathetic step towards the culture of a city that previously had left him disgusted (Acts 17).

In spite of periods of impoverishment and paralysis, the long adventure of church history is one of evolving languages of faith, seeking to embody the gift of God's revelation in tune with the various mentalities of different places and peoples. One needs only to recall the history of Christian art to see how faith has sought out changing mediations that mirror many shifts of sensibility through the centuries. The best chapters of church history witness to many creative efforts to make real, for new situations and cultures, the core reality of God's love in Jesus Christ. And long before the many contemporary debates on this issue, there was a generous awareness that such reaching out called for a distancing of oneself from one's own cultural priorities (and perhaps prejudices). In fact, a famous Roman document of 1659, from the then recently founded Congregation for the Propagation of Faith, gave these blunt instructions for missionaries going to China:

> Do not bring any pressure to bear on these people to change their manners, customs and practices, unless these are obviously contrary to religion and morality. There is nothing more absurd than to want to bring France to China – or to bring Spain or Italy or any part of Europe. Carry none of that but rather faith which neither despises nor destroys the way of life and the customs of any people, when these are not evil

things. On the contrary, faith desires that these traditions be conserved and protected.[4]

A changed horizon

Why are we talking so much about inculturation in these last decades if such sensitivity to local culture was already, at least in wiser moments of church history, a guiding ideal for evangelisation? Because our new horizons of awareness force us to take the diversity of local cultures more seriously than in previous ages. In particular with the arrival of historical consciousness as one of the hallmarks of modern thought, it became impossible to think of any one culture as a permanent or perfect model of life. Once we see the extent to which our ways of thinking and acting are products of history, then we accept more easily the relativity of our languages of living the Christian vision.

Besides, this intellectual insight concerning plurality of cultures has been accompanied by the ending of many colonial regimes as well as by a globalisation process in world communications. As a result the previously unchallenged culture of Europe has begun to see itself as no longer the classical way of 'civilisation', something to be exported and even imposed on less 'advanced' cultures. Without denying the rich heritage of the West, and its unique role in Christian and world history during the second millennium, we need to confess the blind spots of that history: its colonial arrogance and violence, its assumption of inferiority in different ways of life, and its own internal lopsidedness of development (cultivating the scientific and the organisational, a 'masculinist' bias in interpreting life).

Certain forms of mission to foreign cultures are now seen to have been marred by bias – seeing the home language of Christianity as normality and tending to dismiss genuinely spiritual aspects of the receiving culture. The new awareness of inter-culturality offers mutual challenges and helps: in the mirror of 'difference' the previously complacent Western culture can recognise some of its own dehumanising features, or in more Christian terms, the culture can repent of its own sinful structures and admit its need of conversion. What is meant by inculturation is the opposite of that previous insensitivity, but the word is not only awkward but potentially misleading. As Cardinal Ratzinger has put it, 'faith itself is culture', and because there is no such thing as 'pre-cultural or de-cultured Christianity', perhaps a better term would be 'inter-culturality' in order to highlight the 'meeting of cultures' entailed in evangelisation.[5] Ideally the gospel transcends all cultural embodiments but in reality a pure encounter with a culture-free gospel is impossible. Some theologians of inculturation talk as if there were an ahistorical 'essence of christianity' waiting to be incarnated, which 'is to ignore the fact that christianity never existed, not even in its first days, without being expressed in some cultural forms'; instead the adventure of church history always means a 'meeting of cultures in search of a new and original expression of the one faith'.[6] From a different perspective, Christopher Dawson, the historian of religion and culture, looked back at the interactions between faith and barbarianism in Europe in the first millennium and stressed that it was not a matter of easy 'assimilation and permeation, but rather one of contradiction'; interestingly, he added that the key factor in the conversion of the tribes was not the newness of Christian doctrine but the 'new power' of holiness transparent in monastic culture.[7]

Inculturation as crucial to evangelisation

One could give a lot of space to the evolution of the term 'inculturation', tracing its different uses in anthropology and sociology. In those fields (leaving aside the possible distinctions between enculturation, acculturation and so on), the main interest has been in how people are 'socialised', in the sense of learning the ways of the group through a process of social formation. But the details of this background can be left aside because inculturation has now become a specifically theological term, which stresses the reciprocal process involved in communicating the gospel across cultures. Just as the gospel casts new light on each human situation, those situations in turn can bring different dimensions of the gospel into new life.

When this term was adopted in church discourse it was to emphasise that evangelisation, echoing the incarnation itself, demands the insertion of 'the Gospel into the very heart of culture and cultures'.[8] The need for a new, if controversial, term symbolised a new ambition concerning the communication of faith today: not simply adaptation of the language of preaching or worship to the people in question, not only the need for the missionary to understand the cultural context before seeking to communicate the gospel, not even the challenge for the agents of evangelisation to immerse themselves and become genuinely at home in the receiving culture for faith, but rather a different set of sensitivities, priorities and goals in the process of evangelisation.

This new emphasis, captured in the global term inculturation, was born – as already mentioned – from various contemporary insights: (a) a new awareness from anthropology of the dignity and diversity of cultures; (b) from a more developed theology of the presence and action of the Spirit in all cultures; and (c) a recognition that evangelisation is a two-way process of double conversion or mutual enrichment; the faith horizon of the evangeliser is also transformed and challenged through contact with a different culture. All three elements entail a transcendence of attitudes of merely giving-and-receiving, or of more older pastoral strategies. A key hope is that evangelisation can take place from *within* the culture being evangelised. Even before the term 'inculturation' was used in official Catholic statements, Pope Paul VI wrote in 1975 of evangelisation as involving 'transforming humanity from within' (*Evangelii nuntiandi*, No. 18). Thus inculturation involves more than changing a receiving culture from outside: it implies that the gospel will be fully and permanently rooted only when it has been received, felt, celebrated and lived within the deep language of a local culture.

Obviously there is a certain diversity of emphasis within the literature on inculturation. In some theological commentators it can seem to be an ideal goal of integration to be sought and possibly never fully achieved. More often, however, it represents a means to an end, a dimension or stage within evangelisation. For instance the Catholic Bishops of Latin America at their Santo Domingo assembly in 1992 suggested a fourfold movement within which inculturation comes in third place: their text spoke of 'knowledge and discernment of modern culture with a view towards adequate inculturation' and of 'a true inculturation as a way to evangelize culture'.[9] Hence the phases of experience and sifting come first, followed by inculturation, and then the possibility of an evangelised culture. In this model inculturation is seen as a middle term and not an end in itself.

In official Catholic discourse it is fascinating to trace the evolution of insights concerning this field, before and after the first papal use of the term 'inculturation' in 1979. Indeed a quick listing of eight main developments can underline the complex of attitudes required, theologically and spiritually, in order to be involved in authentic inculturation.[10]

1. A first insight stems from a recognition of the *plurality of cultures* (as against the temptation to think of 'our' culture as the norm).

2. Faith is not tied to any one culture and can evolve differently in various cultural settings, *adapting its language* (in a broad sense) to meet local needs.

3. Inculturation will mean a two-way traffic or *mutual enrichment* between two cultural horizons.

4. Instead of being directed by experts from outside, real inculturation will mean transforming a given culture *from within* and hence it involves the entire community.

5. In this light (as will be seen) the incarnation paradigm of embracing human realities needs also the *redemption model of purification* and conversion.

6. Key *criteria for a genuine inculturation* include compatibility with the gospel and unity with the universal Church.

7. The process of *inculturation never finishes* because cultures are in continual evolution and change.

8. Inculturation is not simply a matter for 'mission' territories. The 'new evangelisation' requires a difficult *inculturation of faith in Western cultures* that have largely lost their Christian roots and symbolic memories.

Fourfold theological foundation

If inculturation is an essential part of evangelisation, it is because Christian faith is always more than a private or even personal truth: it is God's vision of way-truth-life, given through Christ in the reality of history. As such, faith is inseparable from a converted way of life in community and in history. Faith that does not promote a healed world remains dead. And if it were possible to have genuine faith in a merely personal way, regardless of society or history, then inculturation would never be necessary. But that kind of faith is not Christian. A faith that does not find shared language of living is a stunted faith: as already seen, a faith that does not 'become culture' is one that is 'not fully lived out'.[11]

In recent years it has become a common practice to link inculturation with four of the fundamental mysteries of faith – creation, incarnation, redemption through the paschal mystery, and Pentecost. Scripture scholars now widely accept that the creation accounts in Genesis were shaped to counter Babylonian myths of origin during the period of the Exile. In this sense the biblical narratives are early examples of dialogue between faith and culture. As against the Babylonian stories of conflict and chaos, Genesis shows God serenely and freely creating as a gift to humanity, and indeed portrays God as an artist rejoicing in the sheer goodness of the finished work. Besides, these texts are much more than stories of origin: they are rooted in a sense of God's continuing relationship with us in our responsibility for the earth, for each other, for human history itself. Creation theology, in this light, is the basis for the long adventure of human culture – symbolised in the mandate to human beings to grow and rule the earth. Thus there is a biblical foundation for seeing culture as *the* human response to God's continuing creative gift, as a co-operation through our freedom with the creator, taking on the whole complex challenge of history, and hence becoming 'fellow-workers with God' (1 Corinthians 3:9).

According to the Brazilian theologian, Mario de França Miranda, God created us as creators of culture but God also created us to share a divine companionship in the drama of healing human history.[12] This double calling offers a rich basis for reflection on inculturation. God's creation continues through us. God as artist works through our free and creative responses. Such a specifically religious vision of the world takes us well beyond the merely functional or political versions of culture that dominate secular thinking today. If God created all that is good, human culture at its best seeks to start from that gift and to build our world with the same freedom and love. Biblically, this is the ideal image, but even within the early chapters of Genesis shadows come, culture turns sour and the results are exile, violence and Babel. This radical ambiguity of human culture points forward to the relevance of the redemption within the process of inculturation.

If creation theology is vital for a biblical perspective on human culture, the incarnation of Jesus Christ is *the* theological basis for inculturation, and this parallel has often been highlighted in church statements and by theologians. When Pope John Paul II first used the term 'inculturation', as already mentioned, in 1979, he spoke of this 'neologism' as expressing well an aspect of the 'great mystery of the Incarnation'. Therefore inculturation imitates, so to speak, that embracing of humanity by God in Christ, in order to give flesh to the gospel again in different cultures.[13]

In a 1995 document that emerged from the special Synod for Africa, entitled *Ecclesia in Africa*, the Pope expands more than in any previous statement on the theological foundations of inculturation, pondering the three mysteries of incarnation, redemption and Pentecost.[14] This text speaks of the incarnation of the Word as 'a mystery which took place in *history*, in clearly defined circumstances of time and space, amidst a people with its own culture'; later it stresses that because the incarnation 'was complete and concrete [it] was also an incarnation in a particular culture' (No. 60). From this analogy with the humanity of Christ comes a theological confidence to appreciate particular cultures as potential languages for the Word; if cultures need Christ for their fullness, in another sense Christ needs cultures in order to continue and complete the gift of the incarnation in different contexts of history. More pastorally, the incarnation analogy offers a double challenge to the evangeliser – to practise a similar descent and to enter fully into the cultural realities of people whom one wishes to evangelise.

However, with the passing of time the incarnation model has

come in for criticism. Nobody denies its basic importance but it has been seen as in need of other complementary dimensions. On its own (and that is the point) to speak of inculturation as echoing the incarnation can seem too complacent and innocent about the struggles involved. Besides, the analogy itself may be misleading insofar as what is inculturated is never the transcendent Word of God but faith, which is always an already inculturated response to God.[15] In official church reflection on inculturation the incarnation model dominated the scene throughout the eighties but in the final decade of the century it was increasingly qualified and complemented by the redemption model. This can be seen in the texts of the Santo Domingo conference of 1992 and in more developed form in *Ecclesia in Africa* (1995).

Hence if inculturation is, in the light of the incarnation, a challenge to the evangelisers, there is another aspect, rooted rather in the mystery of the redemption, where the process of inculturated evangelisation must become a challenge to the 'receiving' culture as well. In this way two elements will be in healthy tension in any process of inculturation: an embracing of human realities and a purification of dehumanising aspects of the culture from within. In the words of *Ecclesia in Africa*, inculturation, which involves both 'insertion' and 'transformation' (No. 59), must 'follow the "logic" proper to the Mystery of the Redemption': every culture 'needs to be transformed by Gospel values in the light of the Paschal Mystery. It is by looking at the Mystery of the Incarnation and of the Redemption that the values and counter-values of cultures are to be discerned' (No. 61). This more prophetic note in the chord of inculturation seeks to do justice to the presence of evil in human history, and to the long struggle of each culture towards Christian authenticity.

Without this link with the cross and resurrection of Jesus, inculturation could remain naively optimistic, or merely a call for more respectful insertion in a given milieu, making oneself all things to all people in order to save them in Christ (cf. 1 Corinthians 9:22). In the light of the redemption inculturation reveals its inevitably conflictual side: culturally entrenched structures of sin are always in need of recognition and of liberation. And if inculturation is to be a mutually enriching process, as insisted upon even as early as

Gaudium et Spes (No. 58), this implies the purification of the faith perspectives of the 'evangeliser' as well. The struggle towards conversion is not simply on the side of the receiver. If the mutuality of inculturation is taken seriously, the culturally conditioned faith embodiments of the Church are also called towards newness and conversion through the interaction with another culture.

One of the imbalances in discussing inculturation is that sometimes the term is so identified with a positive incarnation-emphasis that it comes to mean an entry into cultures without awareness of these calls to transformation on both sides. This can be due to a bending-over-backwards that becomes an 'over-estimation of culture';[16] if so, a certain 'cultural romanticism' creeps in, whereby traditional cultures seem beyond critique and the inevitable tension between the incarnation and redemption dimensions becomes suppressed. On the other hand, the whole inculturation process requires a certain self-sacrifice also on the part of the Church: if the Church is to liberate herself from being linked with any one particular cultural tradition (*Gaudium et Spes*, No. 58 again), the redemption model is an invitation to a self-emptying that echoes the *kenosis* of Christ himself. The ever-difficult balance between an emphasis on new expressions of faith and the need for conversion was expressed in an influential description of inculturation offered by Pedro Arrupe, General of the Jesuits, in 1978:

> Inculturation is the incarnation of christian life and of the christian message in a particular cultural context, in such a way that this experience not only finds expression through elements proper to the culture in question (this alone would be no more than a superficial adaptation), but becomes a principle that animates, directs and unifies the culture, transforming and remaking it so as to bring about 'a new creation'.[17]

Pentecost and plurality

That last expression leads naturally to the fourth analogy – Pentecost. In the comment of *Ecclesia in Africa*, 'all the peoples of the earth . . . profess in their own tongue the one faith in Jesus' as 'the Spirit, who on the natural level in the true source of the wisdom of peoples, leads the Church with a supernatural light into knowledge of the whole truth' (No. 61). There are three main points here: inculturation seeks to echo the miracle of unity in diversity; the Spirit has already been at work in cultures – even before the coming of evangelisation; the Church brings a gift and receives a gift in the process of inculturation.

Pentecost symbolises, in other words, the beginning of a new unification under the Spirit, and instead of the division of Babel, there becomes possible a different relationship between previously fragmented cultures. It is also the moment of the birth of the missionary Church, symbolised by an extraordinary reaching into the languages of diverse cultures.

This Pentecost analogy is of special significance for today's pluralist world. As long ago as the mid-sixties Karl Rahner argued that 'faith has a history of its own, because the absolute self-revelation of God . . . necessarily includes the unlimited possibility of acceptance in a variety of ways'. In other words, every culture and every age in order to remain 'true to the primitive truth' has in fact to 'discover a new form'. It is of the very nature of Christianity to evolve 'the most diverse forms of faith' because of 'widely differing cultures', and there is no guarantee that well-intentioned believers will always arrive at the 'form of faith which is most suitable'.[18] In Rahner's view faith risks self-destruction if it fails to create the forms of faith demanded by a new culture. Long before the term 'inculturation' came into common use, he was pointing to its necessity not just for pastoral reasons but because the dialogue between God's Word and human response always takes places within the flux of history. The ultimate goal of inculturation is reached when a culture is capable of 'self-theologising' and of embodying faith within its own symbolic forms.[19]

Relevant to the post-Christian world?

The avalanche of writing on inculturation within the last two decades has brought out both an old simplicity and a new complexity. It is simple because, at bottom, evangelisation means seeking to reach people's hearts as shaped by the cultures around them. It is complex because so much is entailed in this slow process of pastoral imagination. That complexity is due to various key factors that, as already seen, have come more into focus with the years and which can be gathered under four headings:

1. Cultural consciousness: awareness of the omnipresence of cultural factors fosters a sense of urgency and of delicacy about the goal of evangelising not only individuals but the cultures they inhabit.

2. Universality of the Spirit: a broader theology of divine action in history gives rise to reverence for the goodness present in all cultures and a hope to discern the presence of grace in the lived values and symbols of each people.

3. The challenge of reciprocal discovery: as against the older model of preachers and pagans, the transcultural communication of Christian faith can offer new light on the gospel vision to both 'givers' and 'receivers'.

4. Conversion of horizons: inculturated evangelisation cannot avoid some clash with elements of deception and superficiality that afflict all cultures.

The debates around the topic of inculturation have inevitably been focused on non-Western situations. That is where the issue posed itself most urgently. Does this mean that it is of little or no significance for the so-called Christian West? On the contrary, inculturation is as relevant to First-World countries 'which have been Christianized and now de-Christianized, as it is to the cultures of the Third world in which the Gospel has only recently been proclaimed'.[20] John Paul II has spoken of inculturation as 'the heart, the means and the objective of the new evangelization' (a goal mainly linked to the secularised West).[21] Inculturation therefore needs a difficult retranslation – one might say reinculturation – for the more secularised situations of the Western world. In these post-Christian contexts an 'inculturated evangelization' has the pastoral goal 'to introduce the possibility and reality of God through practical witness and dialogue'.[22]

The same insights apply that have been found necessary in more 'missionary' contexts: the need for sensitivity in reading the hungers of this seemingly secular culture; a trust that the Spirit is at work even in this difficult moment of church history; the quest for appropriate languages of faith to meet the spiritual sensibility of postmodernity; discernment of the various Areopagi of culture in the West; a realisation that mature faith has to root itself within the lifestyles of today; at the same time the gospel has to challenge and transform what is sinful within the dominant culture. In short, the three key invitations of church discourse on this issue have to be imagined anew within the complex cultural context of the West: inculturation of the gospel (a challenge to the Church to forge fresh embodiments of faith in tune with people today); evangelisation of culture (the other side of the coin, whereby the culture itself is challenged into greater authenticity); faith becoming culture (the creation of communities of reflection and commitment that incarnate Christian models of faith for now).

Acknowledging the tensions

Before ending this chapter, it seems right to return to the theme of conflict surrounding inculturation. The theoretical view from the library or desk does not always coincide with the pastoral view from the local situation. As Aylward Shorter put it with admirable clarity, definitions of inculturation 'tend to put the emphasis on one or other term of the equation – Gospel or culture'.[23] Hence even among theologians who comment on this area different dominant vocabularies can be discerned. On the one hand one finds an emphasis on transcendence, proclamation and presence: the gospel transcends all cultures; evangelisation means announcing a truth revealed by God; the Church is the privileged witness of grace in history. All this is true but it can remain idealistic in its distance from the tensions on the ground. Another school of approach tends to highlight the alternative dimensions of historicity, dialogue and mediation: there is no pre-cultural essence of the gospel and all forms of faith are inculturated in their expressions; the relation of faith and culture is not one-way traffic but mutual discovery; the challenge of changing situations is to create credible and fruitful languages of faith. These points are also valid but stem from a quite different pastoral stance. If taken to extremes, the danger of the first school is to reduce inculturation to a strategy of communication, whereas the danger of the second school is to relativise the uniqueness of revelation in Christ.

There are also conflicting voices over the practice of inculturation. For some it can be primarily a question of liturgy. For others such a focus is escapist and the stress falls on the convergence of inculturation and liberation, on the forging of a Kingdom-praxis in tune with local realities often of poverty and oppression. A 'liturgy of life' (Aloysius Pieris) prepares for a liturgy at the altar. Again, political shadows can enter these debates about inculturation. From Africa in particular come questions about what kind of faith was brought by the missionaries of the nineteenth century. Was it perhaps 'a highly spiritualised religion, based on the European secularist world-view that emphasised the separation of religion from the secular earthly sphere of life'?[24] Moreover, if 'culture has not been neutral in South Africa', then talk about inculturation can lend 'itself to manipulation'.[25] An awareness of such questions makes the whole debate more delicate and complex but that is also necessary. Indeed these more controversial voices are rooted in a sense of culture as hiddenly and inevitably conflictual.

The more complacent approaches to inculturation assume an older (pre-postmodern and pre-Girardian) concept of culture derived from anthropology, which sees it as essentially neutral, a matter of what happens to be the way of life around here. However, we are increasingly aware of culture as a subtle battlefield of values and human priorities, with the result that the assumption of neutrality can seem naive or even escapist. In this light, inculturation, with its ambitious hope of evangelising a whole way of life, is seen as 'an extremely difficult process', involving the 'unmasking of cultural domination'.[26] In this whole field honesty demands an admission of tensions and conflicts on many levels, and yet the thrust of inculturation is central for the future of faith in a culturally diverse and yet globalised world.

Chapter Ten

Cultural Discernment

> *We can simultaneously feel bound to plod round the cultural tread-mill yet also brim over with criticism and creativity.* (Margaret Archer)[1]

> *The basic problem with the consumer society is not that it makes us desire too much, but that it makes us desire too little. We are distracted from our true freedom.* (Tony Kelly)[2]

Towards the end of *Pride and Prejudice* Jane Austen offers a beauti-fully barbed critique of nominal Christianity. It occurs when Mr Bennet is reading out a letter from Mr Collins. This social-climbing clergyman is complaining that Mr Collins had received his daughter under his roof even though she had been involved in an irregular relationship: 'You ought certainly to forgive them as a Christian, but never to admit them in your sight, or allow their names to be mentioned in your hearing.' Which provokes Mr Bennet to exclaim ironically, '*That* is his notion of Christian for-giveness!'

It seems a good example of how a culture of respectability can emasculate Christianity, making it fit the common sense of a social group. When that happens the gospel vision becomes 'accultur-ated' instead of 'inculturated'. Mr Collins is not alone in reducing the grit of the Sermon on the Mount to the bias of the tribe. Small though the example is, it seems typical of many cultural forms of pride and prejudice that dilute Christian praxis and can underlie anything from ordinary egoism to structural injustice or even vio-lence. One is forced into a certain humility about the large goals of 'inculturation' or 'faith becoming culture'. 'Evangelization of culture' comes to seem an uphill struggle in each particular moment of history and indeed in each individual life.

One of the pitfalls in talking about faith-and-culture is that the wavelength can remain serenely distant from reality. It can indulge in generalisations or in optimistic visions of synthesis. It can express huge hopes and ideals. And these balloon-like discourses need to be humbled by a blunt 'So what?' How are we to live wisely as Christians within the pressures and complexities of contemporary culture? In raising this question these final chapters approach some of the practicalities of the field, not so much in terms of plans for local action (by their nature they need local knowledge) but by focusing on basic attitudes and options. Pier Paolo Pasolini, the Italian writer and film director, once suggested that in modern culture the Church should go into opposition, much like a political party that loses an election after a long time in power. The question here is about the tone of the opposition. In what spirit should faith view a dominant culture that, either openly or more silently, denies many of the values that are at the core of the Christian vision? The area of disposition is fundamental for discernment, and this chapter will offer variations on the question of how to discern culture.

Unbelief as a cultural product

First, however, it may help to identify some of those blockages to Christian faith that arise within contemporary culture. Years ago I advanced a thesis that has an attractive alliteration: in terms of psychological roots, unbelief takes three main forms – alienation, anger and apathy.[3] That appeared true of the seventies. But now in our new millennium anger is rare; alienation seems in decline; and apathy has come to be the dominant type of unbelief in the Western world. Both anger and alienation are less because they both imply some church contact from which to be alienated or against which to be angry! And there is now a whole new generation of baptised young adults whose formative experiences with religion or church are so thin as to be almost non-existent. Rahner used to speak of 'anonymous Christians'; now we might better speak of 'anonymous unbelievers'. In the words of a Spanish theologian, at present the very 'question of God remains something irrelevant, or even non-existent for the great majority of people.

God is missing but is not missed. This is a genuinely new situation, which never existed before in the world.'[4]

What emerges is that, especially in younger generations, unbelief has become an inherited confusion, a distance from roots, an unaggressive puzzlement about religious practices and their language. As a result they experience unbelief as a cultural by-product. This is no longer de Lubac's 'drama of atheistic humanism' but rather an undramatic limbo of non-belonging. Such a contemporary sense of absence of faith, and the foreignness of its language, is captured in a powerful satiric poem by the Australian, James McAuley, who evokes a whole generation of the religiously 'disinherited':

> Who do not think or dream, deny or doubt,
> But simply don't know what it's all about.[5]

And yet is apathy the whole story now? Even if many young people remain victims of a certain cultural mood, others are moving not only beyond anger but beyond apathy. They may represent a new sensibility of spiritual searching that, as has been seen, is a surprising strand of our postmodernity. The appearance of apathy may only be a mask that conceals a disappointed hunger, but a hunger that is less shy to seek some nourishment and expression than decades ago.

Four forms of cultural unbelief

With this general background, there seem to be four main groupings of culturally rooted unbelief: religious anaemia; secularist marginalisation; anchorless spirituality; and cultural desolation. The first three can be described briefly but the fourth, as a gateway into the major theme of discernment, will need more attention.

'Religious anaemia' covers the many versions of distance from traditional Christian roots, where the fault for the malnutrition lies in a lack of pastoral creativity by the evangelising or educating community. There is not so much a generation gap as a credibility gap of languages, where the typical mediations of Church can be experienced as a foreign tongue. Much discourse about evangelisation may assume the presence of preambles of attitude or disposition that can no longer be taken for granted but have to be created and awoken. In short, religious anaemia is produced when the receiver encounters only the conventional or complacent externals of an institution, and when the communicators of faith fail to enter imaginatively into the culture of the receiver.

Turning to 'secular marginalisation': in recent years there has been an increasing preoccupation that the faith dimension cannot easily make itself heard in any public debate today and that there is a growing tendency to equate democracy with secular liberalism. Especially in the academic and media worlds, a secular culture reigns with the result that religion is subtly ignored as unimportant or as merely a private taste like classical music. Culturally this marginalisation causes a collapse of 'plausibility structures'; as a result a whole interpretation of life comes to appear unreal or unworthy of serious attention.[6] Together these two sources of unbelief produce a profound gap between the culture (both intellectual and lived) and the horizon of faith. The Dutch theologian Anton Houtepen has described the current European situation in eloquent terms:

> God and reference to God have slowly disappeared from consciousness. There is a form of life in which God has been forgotten and . . . there is no longer any need of God . . . The leave-taking of the Christian tradition is not limited to reduced involvement in church life but takes place above all in the forms of daily life that we call culture.

He goes on to say that whereas for believers God is part of their culture, for increasing numbers of people in the West today faith is no longer a lived presence in their culture and this constitutes a far-reaching 'change of consciousness'.[7]

What can be called 'anchorless spirituality' points in an opposite direction and is one of the surprises of postmodernity – the so-called return of the sacred. When people find themselves 'sated but unsatisfied' by the old materialism, as well as bored or untouched by their experience of Church, they can enter a new search without anchors. It is that drifting that constitutes a danger: the hunger is good but insofar as the lived culture weakens people's Christian roots, such a spiritual quest leaves itself open to becoming a mixture of ancient heresies like gnosticism and pelagianism. In a context of religious malnutrition, such lonely spirituality easily becomes another form of dechristianisation. Without community and contemplation, it risks being a narcissism without Christ. In fact this phenomenon seems the product of the two elements already described: where church discourse fails to connect with human needs and where culture forces religious consciousness into the realm of the private, then fundamental spiritual hungers in people remain unsupported and yet desperate in their longing for some kind of food. Thrown back on their own resources, people express their suppressed religiousness in different ways which can range, depending largely on temperament, from so-called New Age explorations to more fundamentalist rigidities. A recent Vatican document, while criticising these phenomena, also sounded a note of self-critique: 'If the Church is not to be accused of being deaf to people's longings, her members need . . . to understand the often-silent cry in people's hearts, which leads them elsewhere if they are not satisfied by the Church.'[8]

The fourth diagnostic is 'cultural desolation', which has already been touched on in the chapter on postmodernity. The key idea is that the pressures of the dominant culture leave many people blocked in a cultural desolation on the level of disposition or readiness for faith. Why? Because it kidnaps their imagination in trivial ways and therefore leaves them unfree for revelation. Or more precisely, for the hearing from which faith comes (cf. Romans 10:17).

Some people bemoan that schools or parishes are not teaching the catechism any more, and that young people leave their education without clear notions of the meaning of Christian faith or church worship. The point has some validity, but is weakened if it implies an exclusively conceptual version of truth, forgetting the impact of a certain cultural conditioning on the level of freedom of disposition rather than doctrine. Hence a first task in this situation is a ministry of disposition, an awakening of the hungers to which the truth may eventually be seen as answer. In this spirit William Barry warns that the 'influence of culture on us escapes our consciousness' and that we need to find 'how any of us encultured human beings can become free enough from our culture to be believers'.[9]

If the main faith blockages today come from cultural desolation on the level of sensibility or readiness for faith, how can we help people towards that consolation or openness where faith can be born? It will mean liberating levels of hearing and of desire that become stifled in the everyday culture. The surrounding culture can be 'dia-bolic' or 'sym-bolic', in the sense of divisive and degrading, or else uniting human potentials into 'togetherness and community'.[10] Before the positive liberation of wonder, a certain negative clearing of the ground may be required. Religious education, for instance, needs to become counter-cultural, in the sense of helping students to identify the dehumanising factors present in lifestyles and assumptions of the culture. To be a Christian today means opting for a certain resistance movement, distancing oneself from the diminished life on offer in the dominant images around. But we need a note of caution here about the tone of our judgements. Too often we can fall into mere moaning about 'isms' (materialism, hedonism, immanentism . . .). Real Christian critique is more than generalised moaning. Discernment is concrete and ultimately positive – in search of genuine life.

It is worth recalling that Cardinal Newman always insisted that unbelief arises not from the intellect but from the state of one's heart, and that the crucial battle zone for faith or unbelief lies in the imagination. In his *Grammar of Assent* he wrote: 'The heart is commonly reached not through the reason, but through the imagination,' adding with typical understatement, 'no man will be a martyr for a conclusion'.[11] As a similar comment on modern culture I value a statement of some fifty years ago by the poet, T. S. Eliot: 'The trouble of the modern age is not merely the inability to believe certain things about God which our forefathers believed, but the inability to feel towards God and man as they did.'[12] This also locates the crisis not in creeds but in sensibility or imagination; it suggests that we have not so much a crisis of faith in the sense of a crisis of creed or message, as a crisis in the *language* or mediations of faith. It is on the pre-conceptual level of intuitive activity – called imagination – that religious meaning is encountered and explored. Indeed 'primordially religion is a function of the creative imagination'.[13]

In this light my thesis about cultural desolation and a resultant lack of freedom for faith situates itself on the level of sensibility. The secular rhythms of culture can kidnap the human imagination into an incapacity to attend to the call of God. When the basic desire for faith is stifled in this way, we have what Buber called an 'eclipse of God'. Perhaps secularism has its most subtle victories in this battleground of imagination – not through outright militancy or violent assault but rather a hijack of the heart into secondaries.

Three Christian responses to culture

If the context is problematic in these ways, how is a Christian to respond wisely to such cultural confusions and pressures? Nobody can answer this question without acknowledging the classic work of H. Richard Niebuhr entitled *Christ and Culture*, with its five models of relationship between faith and culture.[14] However, for present purposes I propose three schools of Christian response to culture: tense hostility; innocent acceptance; discernment and creation of culture. Indeed all three voices may echo within each of us at different times.

Hostility towards the culture

The first tendency – the tense adversary – is one of strongly negative judgement often allied to militant tone. Hamlet-like, this approach sniffs out 'something rotten in the state' of contemporary society and would voice its judgements something like this: 'The culture is simply sick. Trying to view it positively leads only to false compromises. We have lived too long in silence, fearing to speak out about the false turnings in cultural history. A Christian has to be radically suspicious of the deceptions entrenched in such value-shaping worlds as academic life, international politics, the economic system or the entertainment industry. They are secularist and manipulative to the core, even when they pay lip-service to religious or individual freedom. Therefore believers have to protect

themselves from cultural pollution by maintaining strong church
loyalty as a defence against these invading worlds of superficiality.
Only from such a position of clear identity and difference will they
have the authority needed to speak the truth and – even though
faith is by its nature in perpetual opposition – also to begin a
mission to convert the victims of this culture. Against its damage
and multiple fracture, believers have to seek their true identity
within the Church, in order to survive this sophisticated version
of the dark ages.'

It is impossible to deny the grounds for such an evaluation and
there are distinguished Christian thinkers today who would share
this stance. Stanley Hauerwas, for instance, would encourage
believers not to underestimate 'the corruption of our culture' and
its power to tame the Church; hence he stresses the need for faith
to be a confident 'countercultural phenomenon'.[15] It is called first to
recognise the dangers of a woolly liberalism that thinks our
freedom to be self-made, and then to 'replace our culture's convic-
tions' with reasons and fidelities that 'get their power from a
different story' – God's narrative that we do not create or choose.[16]

In less intelligent critiques than those offered by Hauerwas, there
is a risk of hidden fundamentalism and of hostility born of fear.
In its more vehement forms the danger of this approach lies less
in the content than in the tone. Not that all Christian discourse
must be meek and gentle, but it needs to be honest about the
possible desolation behind its dismissiveness. The difficulty with
some armour-plated Christian attitudes towards culture is a question of roots and of fruits. If the roots lack genuine listening or
love for the situation of people, the fruits will be unproductive,
and religion can even come to sound like fanaticism. Even if evils
exist in the culture, sulking and sniping are unworthy as Christian
responses. They often go hand in hand with a separatist tendency
to construct a fortress of church righteousness. Such negative attitudes are understandable as forms of panic and as efforts to
identify the chaos of today in the light of God's revelation and
judgement. But they are flawed insofar as they are grounded in a
non-sympathy for the entire culture of now. Thus these voices
become merely prophets of gloom – a category that Pope John
XXIII chided, firmly and even humorously, at the opening of the

Second Vatican Council, suggesting that he had to listen to too many diatribes about the modern world:

> In the daily exercise of our pastoral office, we sometimes have to listen, much to our regret, to voices of persons who, though burning with zeal, are not endowed with too much sense of discretion or measure. In these modern times they can see nothing but prevarication and ruin. They say that our era, in comparison with past eras, is getting worse, and they behave as though they have learned nothing from history, which is, none the less, the teacher of life . . . We feel we must disagree with those prophets of gloom, who are always forecasting disaster, as though the end of the world were at hand. In the present order of things, Divine Providence is leading us to a new order of human relations.[17]

Innocent acceptance of the culture

The opposite tendency is to be so naive about culture as to be practically unaware of its dangers; it can be recognised in at least three forms – passive resignation, thoughtless secularisation, and indiscriminate embracing of pluralism.

To fall into passive resignation means to abandon any attempt to influence the culture or to create alternatives. This position might well share some of the negative judgements of the 'adversary' position but, instead of attacking, it tends to throw in the sponge about making any impact on the surrounding world. Everything seems so complex that one cannot hope to make any difference, and hence it seems wiser to cultivate one's own back garden, so to speak. This means retreating into non-contact with the culture, leaving that culture unchallenged in its control of people's imaginations and hearts.

Another possible version of this acceptance of the culture involves an unreflected 'buying into' the dominant values. Looking back now at some of the 'renewal' of religious life or of liturgy that took place in the decade after the Second Vatican Council, it can be asked whether it did not embrace a certain secularisation too rapidly. In those overdue and necessary efforts at pastoral relevance, one could hold that valuable aspects of tradition were

unwisely discarded. Even to raise this issue can seem 'resto-
rationist', as if wanting to put the clock back. But it need not be
so. In the urgency to emerge from the excessively closed culture
of pre-conciliar Catholicism, a certain 'acculturation' seems to have
taken place: the influence of the secular liberalism of the sixties
caused such an unbalanced emphasis on individual expression that
genuine elements of Christian anthropology were abandoned. It is
not just a superficial question of religious dress or of folk music in
the liturgy: these are transitory and secondary issues. More serious
was an undervaluing of symbolic languages for the sacred or an
insensitivity to the need for some counter-cultural structures if
spirituality is to survive. Ultimately at stake was the inescapable
differentness of the gospel way: it transcends common sense, challenges all merely human values to conversion and creates an
inevitable tension with the assumptions of a non-religious culture.
In this light, some of the undiscerning assimilation of the anti-
structural, anti-symbolic and anti-spiritual culture of the sixties
now seems to be an example of 'innocent acceptance'.

A third source of weakness before the dominant culture comes
from certain interpretations of 'pluralism'. Plurality of lifestyles
and meanings exists all around us and pluralism is a response to
that complex reality. A valid pluralism recognises the rights of
other people even if it does not necessarily agree with their values.
But some versions of cultural pluralism do not grasp that distinction and hence the values themselves topple over into relativism.
If 'one culture is as good as the next', then there is no need for
discernment of cultural practices.[18] An indiscriminate pluralism
would abdicate any possibility of evaluating cultures. Its mistake
is to slide from an acknowledgement of diversity and of rights to
freedom into a hazy attitude whereby all cultural embodiments
are equally valuable in their own way. But is it true? This soft kind
of pluralism usually goes hand in hand with a 'coherence' rather
than a 'referential' theory of truth; if there is only 'truth-within-a-
system', then we have no yardstick for cultural discernment.

Discernment of dispositions

It is healthy, if somewhat uncomfortable, to look into these mirrors of naive anger or naive liberalism; it prepares the ground for a more genuine discernment of culture and shows that we need another wavelength of response. In this respect one can ponder the most relevant moment in the New Testament for this whole theme. Chapter 17 of the Acts of the Apostles offers a classic case of contrasting responses to the surrounding culture. St Paul's discourse on the Areopagus is often cited as the greatest New Testament example of a positive outreach to pagan culture and of the possible harmony between human aspirations and the revelation-event of Jesus Christ. But what is less frequently noted is that the generosity of his speech differs greatly from his own initial reactions to Athens. The account of his stay in the city begins with an unusually strong expression of negativity: 'his whole soul was revolted at the sight of a city given over to idolatry' (Acts 17:16). Indeed the Lucan introduction goes out of its way to stress the difficulties of reaching such a sophisticated but superficial culture, one that sneered at Paul as a 'parrot' and indulged itself in the latest ideas on the level of fads and mere entertainment.

It is all the more remarkable, therefore, that the Areopagus speech should open by praising the Athenians for being so religious and that Paul should now interpret an altar to an Unknown God, not as idolatry, but as a sign that the Athenians had genuine religious hungers and were worshipping God without fully knowing the One whom Paul came to announce. The remainder of his speech continues to obey the pastoral principle of making himself 'all things to all' types of people in order to reach them with the good news (1 Corinthians 9:22). Paul gradually moves from external images to evoke the transcendence of God beyond all images. He gives special attention to the fundamental human experience of desire for God: people feel their way towards God, whereas in fact God is not far from anyone because in God 'we live and move and exist' (Acts 17:28). That last phrase is borrowed from a Greek poet – yet another symbol of the effort to enter into the culture and to invite people to faith from within their deepest values. Paul then seeks to move on from evoking

human awe before creation to the need for repentance as the only
way to leave ignorance behind. Of course this attempt at reaching
Athenian culture ends in relative failure. People laugh at the
mention of resurrection from the dead, but some postpone judgement, promising to hear him again, and some are converted.
Indeed the text gives their names as if to highlight that fact.[19]

Paul's change of attitude from disgust with the culture to identifying seeds of the gospel within pagan religiousness seems a
perfect example of the contrast between desolation and consolation
that underlies all discernment. Contact with a new culture can
easily provoke judgemental and negative reactions. Differentness
causes fear. The externals may seem decadent. The behaviour of
people can appear superficial and astray. But does that judgement
stem from a certain desolation of attitude, a distrusting that the
Spirit could be present within this cultural situation in any way?
If so, the freedom to discern is not yet present. How did Paul move
from disgust to generosity? Perhaps he prayed as he climbed the
hill to the Areopagus. At all events he arrived at a more positive
intuition into the values of Athenian culture. Behind the frivolous
appearances lay deeper spiritual hungers. Behind the games of
argumentativeness lay a poetry and a spirituality that he began to
appreciate in a new way. Paul's whole disposition seemed to have
undergone a sea change; such a graced conversion of attitude is a
key to any Christian discernment of culture. We need to move from
desolation of judgement to a discernment rooted in consolation.
Otherwise we are in danger of seeing only the 'flatter and shal-
lower forms' all too visible around us, and miss the 'higher and
fuller modes of authenticity' that are also present as key characteristics of our culture.[20]

Many church documents advocate a careful 'discernment' of the
cultural influences surrounding us today but these texts give few
if any indications about how to practise such discernment. To fill
this gap, even in a sketchy way, the next few paragraphs here
will draw on the tradition of spiritual discernment, especially that
associated with St Ignatius of Loyola, seeking to adapt its per-
sonalist approach to the complex questions of interpreting our
culture. In this light, discernment will be seen as a specifically
Christian way of reading reality. It aims at more than a human

sifting of the shadows and lights in a social environment. Discernment does not neglect any human instruments for cultural analysis but it seeks to recognise the presence of the Spirit within the human. It enlarges the method of 'reading' a situation from description of outer factors to reflection first on the deeper attitudes of people.

For the sake of clarity, let me propose a summary of the art of discernment – as involving three Ds.

- To recognise the Spirit we need a *disposition* of openness and freedom to be surprised. It requires 'eyes of faith' and an avoidance of mere demonising or prejudiced evaluations (such as St Paul's initial reaction to Athens). It rests on a trust that God's revelation continues and can be perceived in our responses to the situations around us.
- To discern any cultural phenomenon, such as contemporary globalisation, we need to ask about the *direction* in which it moves people's hearts and lives. Is it leading us towards what is humanising, or is it crushing our freedom and closing us to compassion? What dimensions of our humanity are being silenced or ignored by the iron law of the so-called free market?
- Thirdly, discernment exists not just for interpretation but for *decision*: it is a path towards lived priorities and commitments. Its hope is to ensure the Christian quality of our choices. What options do we need to make in order to reshape our global connections as sources of life for our planet and especially for the poor? What practices could embody a Christian way of life within today's cultural complexity?

In short, this art of discernment is dispositional, directional and decisional. It asks 'What is really going on?', not superficially but in the depths of our cultures. It offers a religious basis for what is called 'cultural agency'. In an attractive image of St Gregory the Great, from the first Christian millennium, for good discernment you need a large nose, to distinguish good and bad odours. A small nose, he argued, would not be enough. A small nose, in our circumstances, would be any cultural analysis that offered only an external balance sheet. We need contemporary versions of those ancient skills of discernment in order to listen to the 'whence' and the 'whither' of what is happening. If the Spirit is at work, then the good fruits will show themselves. If Mammon is in charge, then sooner or later the results will prove sour. Towards what is our imagination being moved? That is a key question for spiritual discernment. It asks about the flow of our lives as a 'whither': is the impact of culture fostering a generous flow of openness or pushing us towards what is imprisoning and insensitive to the world's pain? One direction is called consolation, the other desolation. Consolation therefore is not just a matter of 'feeling good' or of cultivating 'positive thinking'; it is a faith-based experience, a sense of expanding in harmony with what is deepest in us, the Spirit in us. In large options and in small reactions, consolation is an experience of being-in-tune-with-Christ and of moving towards gospel vision and values. Desolation is the contrary experience of disharmony, disconnection, distance, distrust perhaps of everything and everyone. It is more a matter of paralysis than of positive movement. Consolation is like open hands, ready to receive. Desolation is like closed fists, ready to reject.

A transformed agenda of interpretation

To practise this specifically Christian way for reading cultures involves a major shift of agenda from describing external influences and trends, or listing the pros and cons of a given situation. It aims at identifying the deeper responses the culture provokes in us and indeed in whole communities of Christians. Earlier I stressed cultural desolation as a source of blockage against faith. But faced with the sheer weight of that desolation around us, agents of the gospel may fall into a different desolation of attitude. Beyond mere hostility and beyond naive acceptance, there is the call to discern the culture with consolation, to move like St Paul from understandable disgust to a disposition of hope, rooted in the Spirit.

Without such a starting point in consolation, one is in danger of rejecting entire ways of life as utterly beyond the reach of the gospel. Of course negative judgement may be an appropriate response to important aspects of the dominant culture. The call to ground oneself in a certain consolation does not close the door to prophetic denunciation of what may be dehumanising. Paradoxically we need to be able to see the desolations induced by the culture while guarding consolation as the ground of our Christian response, because to see desolation only with desolation is a formula for negativity. If that happens, one can become incapable of discerning any seeds of goodness. Indeed St Paul's initial reaction to Athens may well have been an example of viewing outer desolation with inner desolation.

So there can be no real discernment of culture without consolation as basic attitude, as a tone and trust that liberates our disposition to understand with something of the wisdom of God. Consolation does not mean rose-tinted viewing. In fact it involves a double expectation: there will be conflict, ambiguity, anti-values enthroned, but there will also be signs of hope and of real hunger, fruits of the Spirit. No situation is beyond redemption. Judge we must, but in a spirit of discernment, even of aggressive discernment, but never in a tone of dismissiveness. Some negative evaluations are inevitable – otherwise we would be innocent about evil and oppression. But blanket rejections of contemporary culture seem both wrong and useless. Once the disposition is right, it does not mean that the process of discerning a culture is easy. Charles Taylor has spoken of such discernment as a struggle, warning that we might 'not be sufficiently bewildered, that we think we have it all figured out from the start, and we know what to affirm and what to deny'.[21]

Discernment of culture, then, hinges on one's own spiritual disposition, and the resultant tone of one's dialogue with the culture. If desolation rules, a fairly fruitless tone of blanket moaning about reality can take over. If consolation is arrived at, critique of the falsities of the culture will be expressed in concrete ways, accompanied by a trust that these shadows are not the whole story: consolation means acknowledging that there are also authentic values within the culture which need liberating from the deceptions. Consolation breaks the negative magnifying glass that can only see decadence or disaster. Consolation is like that moment at the end of John's gospel where the disciples recognise the Lord on the shore after a night of total failure. Consolation is what liberated St Paul to glimpse the spirituality hidden behind the idolatry. In other words, consolation trusts that God is already present and somehow creative in all human cultures: therefore 'we are in consolation when we are fully in touch with what God is doing in our hearts' and when we try to 'bring to light the character of God's activity in those cultures' where we minister.[22] Discernment ultimately means sharing that conversion of disposition of St Paul in Athens, and thus being able to recognise smoke signals of hope rising from what may at first seem like a burnt-out desert.

Chapter Eleven

Cultural Consciousness in Faith Ministry

> *Culture is the greatest and most overlooked educational influence in most lives.* (Michael Warren)[1]

> *The current challenge in youth ministry is not religious but anthropological: it is about who they are becoming. This question of identity requires a prior critique of the manipulative images in the dominant culture.* (Riccardo Tonelli)[2]

To evoke the mixture of damaged imagination and spiritual desire that characterises many younger searchers of today, we can draw on two authors from North America. Douglas Porpora is a Christian sociologist and Douglas Coupland is a bestselling Canadian novelist with a large following among the young generation. Both of them describe contemporary 'landscapes of the soul' in terms of a painful loss of meaning, except that Coupland's narratives often lead his readers through chaos to a clearing in the forest, where some healed hope is glimpsed. In Porpora's words, 'we have lost touch with a whole range of moral and spiritual emotions' and as a result God has 'become emotionally remote'.[3] In his view the key issue is not erosion of faith or belief in itself; a deeper challenge comes from the fact that desire or concern for religious meaning has faded under the impact of an alienating consumer culture. This interpretation is in tune with what I earlier called a postmodern crisis of imagination, disposition or sensibility. In Porpora's view the sense of moral purpose has withered on the level of shared feeling, in spite of the fact that surveys show that over 50 per cent of Americans assign God considerable importance in their lives. The problem is to find a spiritual quality of faith that can survive and even flourish within the new complexity of culture.

Coupland's characters, by contrast, are a generation raised without religion, and yet his typical plot concerns a quest for spiritual vision on the part of young rebels frustrated with the dominant lifestyle. He has even been called the John Bunyan of postmodernity. The quasi-religious language of his stories is surprisingly overt, as a selection from *Girlfriend in a Coma* can illustrate.

> Ask 'a few questions and suddenly you realize that they're despairing about the world – that the confidence is a mask'.

> 'You're right to be thinking of your souls – the better part of you.'

> 'You think you've been forsaken – that the opportunity for holiness is gone, but this isn't true.'

> 'We will change minds and souls from stone and plastic into linen and gold.'[4]

It would be easy to dismiss this as New Age froth but there is an honest openness here and in this sense Coupland's books symbolise what we called the positive sensibility of postmodernity. He voices post-materialist hungers with eloquence and sometimes with moving simplicity. The prayer-style ending of *Life after God* has often been quoted:

> My secret is that I need God – that I am sick and can no longer make it alone. I need God to help me give, because I no longer seem to be capable of giving; to help me be kind, as I no longer seem capable of kindness; to help me love, as I seem beyond being able to love.[5]

This moment, which involves a baptismal-like immersion in cold water, is all the more powerful in its humility because of the chaotic nature of the adventures of these stories. After cultural fragmentation comes the possibility of healing simplicity. It seems to be one of the new and potentially hopeful notes within youthful postmodernity today. Of course one has to add that this cultural trend is not favourable to church forms of religion. Even though it 'shows a fascination with experience at the nexus of the human and the divine', it is certainly marked by ambiguity and 'instability'.[6]

In general, however, the spiritual identikit picture of young people offered by many sociologists in Europe and North America is fairly bleak. They tend to present the young person of today as living within a restricted horizon of meaning and values. The typical quest is subjective rather than political, staying safely within the private sphere of relationships rather than confronting the larger world of social commitments or life-projects. The 'drivers' or goals remain largely pragmatic and consumeristic – a good job, the freedom that comes with money, perhaps a small family. For a generation that lacks models to follow, an adolescent phase of non-commitment can now extend itself into their late twenties or further. A psychology of 'weak identity' is said to be pervasive, in the sense of feeling themselves impotent before the large forces that govern society. This tendency to abdicate from large issues or to withdraw into a narcissistic space goes hand in hand with relativism over truth and morality. Truth becomes immanent – only what-makes-sense-to-me counts. Conscience is viewed as infallible, in the sense of whatever feels 'OK' to the isolated self.

But to say all this is only half the story. Apart from the more searching spirit evoked by Coupland, simply to accept this description of a generation is to forget that cultural trends do not happen without cause. Behind the present confusion and adriftness lies a culture of images that has educated this age group more powerfully than at any previous time in history. It is one thing to put together elements of such an identikit picture. It is another, and more urgent, task to discern the roots of these characteristics in the pressures of a culture. More important still is to find ways of liberating people from the imprisonment of living as passive products of this culture. Insofar as they buy into the surrounding norms they become handicapped: victims of their context, increasingly incapable of questioning the assumptions they have unconsciously absorbed from their environment. In this respect an Italian philosopher, Massimo Cacciari, voices his irritation with Church-based complaints about relativism in the culture. Instead of relativism we are suffering, in his view, from a cultural hegemony where in fact only one set of influences holds sway: a combination of technical and economic mindsets links up with a closed individualism in order to produce a new empire of banality.[7] If this is so, then the new generations are particularly vulnerable to the impact of this subtle dictatorship, especially through the impact of the 'global culture industries'. In a provocative book the political scientist Michael Budde accuses Catholic leaders of innocence on this point: they discuss the cultural influence of the media, hoping that they can serve gospel values, without recognising the extent to which this 'systemic' structure remains in thrall to money-making. Rather like Hauerwas, as cited in our previous chapter, Budde calls for 'a reclaimed awareness of the differences being Church should entail'.[8]

Issues for youth ministry

In the light of these horizons, the Cinderella story of the emergence of culture onto centre stage is echoed today in the field of youth ministry. Indeed, without alertness to the cultural context, pastoral work with the younger generations is in danger of having only a marginal impact. The reason is not hard to find: the key curriculum in the lives of young people is not school or church, or even home after a certain age, but media culture and the zone of relationships. The fact that it is a hidden curriculum only increases its power and makes religious efforts to reach young people irrelevant unless they pay explicit attention to the surrounding cultural influences.

Against this background the history of youth ministry in recent decades is one of tension between different perspectives. In particular, the period of the seventies saw three approaches in rivalry with one another. One school was 'experiential' or existential, stressing the centrality of searching that started from young people themselves; unless evangelisation paid attention to their felt needs and questions it would not prove fruitful. A second approach defended the continuing importance of 'content'; unless the teacher or preacher clarified the meaning of the creed and of church practices, the intellectual basis for faith would be absent. A third response highlighted 'community'; unless young people found opportunities for sharing and belonging, for spaces of learning practices, they would never survive as believers amid the complex pressures of today.

All three tendencies had their own validity but all of them remained somewhat innocent of the power of the emerging youth cultures. Of course these influences were not entirely negative. In spite of manipulation and superficiality, the youth cultures can be found to have their own sensibility to gospel values; much church discourse can waste its energy in negativity – scapegoating 'pop music' for instance. Such generalised moaning belongs to the 'adversary' family of response described earlier, and lacks the precision of the real critique needed. The mass media may indeed be a source of triviality and apathy, and pop music can certainly be associated with mindless hedonism, but blanket condemnations cut little ice, particularly with young people. They can even feel it – from elders – as an insensitive dismissal of one of their natural environments and languages.

Within recent decades youth ministry has come to see the centrality of cultural discernment, but only as part of a larger convergence of responses. The three emphases just mentioned retain their importance but within a wider set of approaches – more developmental, more spiritual and more cultural.

'Developmental' includes all those insights into the slow process of possible Christian maturity: it draws on the wisdom of 'initiation' stages in the catechesis of the early centuries, and it sees young people in particular as being on a delicate journey of seeking and finding meaning for their lives. A gradualist understanding of youth ministry recognises what growth points are ripe and what forms of faith are for the moment out of reach. Hence the interpersonal language that dominated some thinking in the seventies is now seen more as a necessary but incomplete stage of faith development. To foster only an interpersonal agenda could be a subtle form of stunted maturity, and one that will not last into adulthood. Indeed it is one of the temptations of contemporary culture to limit reality to the field of relationships, falling into what Richard Sennett terms 'the ideology of intimacy',[9] and avoiding tougher questions about social justice and about the larger forces at work in culture.

'Spirituality' has become, as already mentioned, a surprisingly central word in today's culture. It is evidence of a certain desperation for inner roots, or, more positively, of a rediscovery of non-materialistic values – of silence and wonder, of qualities of heart-listening, of capacities for contemplative depth, ultimately a new hunger for genuine languages of personal prayer. Youth ministry has found that skills of stillness can be taught and that many young people can only arrive at some maturity of faith decision if they learn to listen to the Spirit in these quieter ways. But this dimension is not without its cultural deceptions: within youth culture narcissistic versions of 'New Age' spirituality can prove attractive, and result in a pseudo-spiritual cul-de-sac, meeting only those cultural tendencies to want transcendence on the cheap. Hence discernment of culture is particularly crucial, to protect the spiritual journey from mere self-exploration and to allow it to become a challenging encounter with the gospel.

Youth ministry has moved from the tensions between the schools of experience, content and community to include developmental and spiritual approaches, but 'cultural discernment' can be argued to be the most ambitious and difficult goal of youth ministry as understood today. As guides to this dimension of reflection on contemporary culture, I draw here on the works of Michael Warren and John Kavanaugh. Both authors focus on North American culture, Warren often from the point of view of communications and youth ministry, and Kavanaugh more from the perspective of a philosopher with a keen eye for social trends and the need for a spirituality of resistance today. Independently of one another, both have developed a style of aggressive discernment of culture. 'Aggressive' should not be interpreted as putting them into the camp of the 'tense adversaries'; it means rather that they argue forcefully against being too innocent about cultural control and oppression today. They both see such oppression as undermining, not so much Christian faith in itself, as the very possibility of believing – especially among the younger generations. To cite the phrase of St Paul once more, if 'faith comes from hearing', what in contemporary culture induces spiritual deafness? In this sense their work is a diagnosis of the causes of faith-deafness, not only in the general attitudes but in the lived 'practices' of our culture.

Warren's approach to culture is much influenced by Raymond Williams' insistence (examined in chapter 1) that culture is not just a field of passive influences that happen to happen, but rather a signifying system for the 'production' of meaning. If culture involves patterns of interpreting reality, 'people do not so much believe in their society's patterns of thought and feeling; they approach life by means of them'.[10] In this way culture offers images that become the unnoticed and pre-reflective paradigms people live by. Kavanaugh sees American culture as involving a clash between two sets of values – even though the battle zones are not always recognised. 'These competing life-forms can be expressed as the "gospels" of Personhood and Commodity.'[11] On the one hand there is the Christian vision of life as relationship or covenant between persons; on the other hand there is the idolatry of possessions, which undermines personhood and reduces even interpersonal areas of life to 'dominance and self-aggrandisement'.[12] More recently Kavanaugh has commented that 'a profoundly narcissistic utilitarianism' infects ethical thinking on issues as diverse (but connected) as war, abortion and euthanasia.[13] If the reality system, which shapes our assumptions and priorities, is depersonalised in this way, the culture truly becomes an anti-culture. Where Mammon is the hidden god, we suppress whole ranges of our humanity and become invulnerable spectators shielded from the cries of pain around us.

Behind the typical 'habits of the heart' both authors see the pressures of politics and economics: the culture has identifiable roots in social forces that control our perceptions, and as in the case of advertising, do so with deliberate skill and foresight. One of Warren's key insights is that faith today cannot reach any healthy aliveness without awakening to the cultural curriculum that shapes people's attitudes into certain 'structures of feeling' (an expression from Williams). What is at stake here is an undermining of freedom for faith, and a resultant unreadiness for the gospel: against this imprisonment or unawareness 'coming to see that one has a way of seeing involves a shift in consciousness'.[14] Similarly for Kavanaugh a first step towards a Christian option of life entails realising the pervasiveness of the commodity philosophy and the lived atheism that it assumes and promotes: only then can one come to recognise inevitable 'oppositions between cultural wisdom and Christian wisdom'.[15]

In an article with the indicative title 'The Material Conditions of

Our Seeing and Perceiving', Warren highlights that the cultural space around us is far from neutral territory. It is full of messages that invite us to imitate various lifestyles and that seek to shape our consciousness. If religious reflection forgets these factors, it will simply 'collude in enabling the conditions of our seeing to go unnoticed'.[16] If the power of 'today's communications media to shape our worldview and values according to the interest of consumerism is alarming',[17] a first step is simply to become aware of the impact of social images and hence to have a shield against the cultural coding that tries to manipulate attitudes.

Possibility of cultural agency

This awakening to a possible tyranny of images is only an initial stage in any cultural discernment. Warren and Kavanaugh are in agreement that some creative alternative is needed, in the form of Christian communities of lived resistance to the dominant culture. In this sense theoretical critique is not enough: more is needed than, for example, identifying the deceptions of consumerist values. Unless the Church moves towards being a producer of meaning, its discernment will remain passive. Faith-based communities must move towards 'cultural agency' because 'a religious culture of resistance is impossible unless it is grounded in patterned ways of living that embody an alternative vision of life'.[18] In today's cultural complexity it is self-defeating to think of evangelisation as only a matter of communicating a 'message': it is also about the conditions of the practice of the Christian vision.

Hence the living out of alternative visions within community is the only effective critique of the triviality fostered by the dominant culture: 'A vision of life is not verified so much by its truth claims as in the life practice it fosters or produces.'[19] Warren likes to use the expression 'life structures' to point to a crucial area of cultural danger and of potential cultural resistance. It indicates an accumulation of daily choices, akin to what Rahner calls a 'fundamental option': it also suggests a pattern of habits and attitudes that do not easily change. The dominant culture pushes us towards egoist patterns; Christian faith aims at a radically different culture of self-transcendence and self-giving, which needs cultural incarnation as 'a gospel-based way of life in communities'.[20] To embody forms of Christian holiness for today's culture requires a special kind of community that avoids the trap of self-concern through 'individualized life-commitment, prayer, and the outreach to service'.[21] In brief, if young people (or believers of any age) are to survive against the subtle undermining forces of a superficial culture, it means recognising the battleground and developing skills of shared resistance. These skills will necessarily involve 'structures' and 'practices', in the sense of definite roads of growth and definite activities or commitments. And, as Warren insists, only in community will we find the strength to see through the silliness and to forge alternative languages of life.

The gospel saying that nobody can serve two masters finds its field of cultural conflict today on the level of human imagination, as a battle between different sets of symbols about what makes life worth living. Even the film *The Matrix* (and its less impressive sequel) raises these questions: whether we can be unconsciously programmed by a system that surrounds us and how we might choose to resist it. A good way of alerting young people to this battle zone would be to ask them, 'Who is imaging your life for you?' Or else, 'Who is telling you stories that claim to show reality?' Christianity was always a story-telling and imagination-transforming vision. In many countries now children spend more time watching television than they spend in school; since most of them glean their images of the 'good life' from television, faith is faced not just with a secularising force in the sitting room, but with a challenge to retell the Christian stories in ways that can rival the egoist myths. The idols of cultural imperialism need not only unmasking but rivalling and replacing.

In this respect Warren remains suspicious of various religious commentators on the mass media who look on them as a new instrument for communicating faith values; they can ignore the extent to which the media are totally 'embedded' in a commercially oriented world, a world expert in selling both products and attitudes through the bait of entertainment. This kind of culture is not genuinely 'of the people' but rather 'concocted for the consumption of the people'.[22] Media of this kind do not constitute a neutral instrument that needs only to be well used in order to produce good Christian fruit. If the roots of the tree are sick, the fruit cannot be untainted.

Do structures of sin inevitably underlie many expressions of popular culture? Even to pose such a question could seem to put one into the camp of the 'tense adversary', judgemental and dismissive of culture. But to shrug off the validity of the question puts one into the other extreme of the 'innocent accepter' who thinks everything is potentially good. How can we move beyond these inadequate stances towards seeing what Christian discernment entails? The example of television is a test case. Its more superficial productions unashamedly kidnap and colonise human attention with a fast-moving world of appearances. At its average worst, television both fosters and assumes an uncritical passivity in its public. But in this respect it is a symbol and summary of all that is potentially dehumanising in contemporary culture: it may only be the tip of the iceberg of false consciousness and of entrenched anti-culture. If so, some critical alertness will be a crucial first step towards cultural discernment, but Christian commitment calls for something more vigorous and creative.

Building life structures

Cultural discernment has two phases, one of interpretation and judgement, and the other of communal spirituality and creation of Christian life structures. Together the two stages amount to that cultural agency whereby 'a person decides to exercise some judgment and control over the kinds of cultural material she/he will accept and the kinds that must be resisted'. Such agency will not only involve making reflective choices about 'the meanings and values created for us' in a given culture but active ways of 'examining and judging the *channels* by which these meanings and values are communicated to us'.[23] This means asking questions about power and about who benefits from the cultural situation as it is. We need a more penetrating level of inquiry merely describing the cultural traits that happen to be dominant. They never just happen to be dominant, and this more aggressive discernment wants to know what is really dominant and *why*.

What can be done to counter the widespread dehumanisation?

If Warren and Kavanaugh are forceful in their negative critique of cultural oppressions and equally strong in their advocacy of cultural agency, they both seem hopeful about the potential of faith-rooted communities as sources of cultural discernment – on certain conditions. Church life in practice can fall into cowardly reproduction of the bias enthroned in the surrounding culture. But the prophetic call is to the opposite of such passive assimilation. We return to the idea that gives a title to this book: that a clash between cultures is inevitable, not always a clash of confrontation and total conflict, but a clash of two loyalties, an ambiguous set of influences to be sifted with spiritual wisdom. And such discernment is an essential gift of the religious imagination, because it seeks out the signs of love and self-giving that – in the Christian vision – are ultimately empowered by Christ but that are present as seeds in all that is good in human experience.

Particular tensions arise when church institutions become servants or instruments of the wider culture. Instead of authentic inculturation, there is a real danger of what Kavanaugh calls 'acculturation' – in the sense of being absorbed in a compromising way into the dominant culture, thus losing its salt, as the gospel puts it. Without constant self-critique the Church can 'become too comfortable with Caesar' instead of subverting the domination of the 'commodity kingdom': 'If the Christian does feel at home, something is drastically wrong.'[24] An obvious example here is the Catholic school. Clearly the relation between the official faith-vision of the school and the unofficial cultural agenda lived in the daily praxis of both school and society will seldom be a matter of 'sweetness and light' (as Arnold said in his humanistic view of culture). The Christian ideals of the institution may be subtly hijacked by the pressures of competition (from examinations to sport) or from the alternative curriculum of liberal relativism and self-fulfilment that is so easily absorbed from the wider culture. In this way youth ministry or religious schooling can fall into what Warren calls a 'Jesus reduction program', offering a soft picture of Christ that 'neatly fits the aspirations of middle-class' culture.[25]

However, if one points an accusing finger at the culture and its power to kidnap church energies, in all justice one should equally put church practices into the dock: the way the community acts can be a source of self-deception and of stunted conversion. Unless young people and lay people are given voice and power to participate in the formation of church life, the Church itself is in danger of cultivating exactly the passivity that it might criticise in the surrounding culture. It is not enough to be asked to foster 'reproduction of religious meaning'; each generation needs to forge an 'original production' of the Christian vision.[26] It is worth adding that support for this line of thinking can be found, perhaps surprisingly, in Ludwig Wittgenstein's later notebooks. There he remarks that religious belief must be 'something like a passionate commitment' that can only be taught in the 'form of a portrayal'. Turning to the question of how to educate people towards faith, the great philosopher writes: 'It would be as though someone were first to let me see the hopelessness of my situation and then show me the means of rescue until, of my own accord, or not at any rate led to it by my *instructors*, I ran to it and grasped it.'[27]

Wittgenstein would start youth ministry (an expression he never heard of!) with a diagnosis of need and follow up with a presentation of a way of life in full flow. Similarly this chapter has insisted that the only fruitful answers to the seductive power of the culture will come when Christian faith is lived together with creativity and energy. There is a battle for people's minds and hearts and imaginations. Individuals need the support of communities to forge a Christian option that can survive. They also need a spirituality in the wide sense of a whole way of life that nourishes Christian commitment. But if a spirituality of cultural resistance is not simply a matter of prayer alone, prayer nevertheless is a 'counter-cultural act': 'it is a reappropriation of our personhood and identity'.[28] Since 'entire cultures and traditions can be wrong', faith ministry needs a new stress on 'self-ownership'.[29] Against the complexity of the cultural pressures today, only a convergence of Christian skills of resistance will bear fruit. To imagine some of those possibilities will be the topic of the final chapter.

Chapter Twelve

Towards a Spirituality of Culture

*Spirituality, the self's experience before God, occurs in history . . .
in the forms and ways of seeing of a given culture.* (Veronica Brady)[1]

*Spirituality, in its manifold forms, is about receiving energy for
life . . . It is lived and sought in community and for others.*
(World Council of Churches, Canberra Assembly, 1991)[2]

A poem by Seamus Heaney can offer an evocative opening for
these final reflections. The title itself is significant: 'In Illo Tempore'
('at that time') used to be the opening words for the gospel reading
in the Latin Mass. And the poem evokes an older world of satur-
ating symbols and sacraments:

> The big missal splayed
> and dangled silky ribbons
> of emerald and purple and watery white.
> Intransitively we would assist,
> confess, receive.

A stanza later that communal 'we' changes to a lonely 'I' walking
at night beside the sea:

> and even the range wall of the promenade
> that I press down on for conviction
> hardly tempts me to credit it.[3]

This captures something of the cultural-cum-religious change of
these decades and the typical collapse of old securities, especially
in Ireland. Only a generation ago, Catholicism meant largely that
tighter universe or quasi-sacral community. We have since passed
through a disturbing period of insecurity, but in recent years we
may be reaching a new sensibility. Indeed in a recent interview
Seamus Heaney has remarked that our urge to secularise our lives

was a mistake; he now insists more on the need to 'credit marvels'
and to revisit thresholds of the spirit.

In an anchored world of pre-modernity religion permeated
culture, so much so that a religious culture seemed the only conceivable horizon of existence. When that habitual sense of the
sacred disappears, either faith becomes a decision taken against
the tide, or else it falls into that lostness imaged in Heaney's
nocturnal walk on the beach. Granted these radical transformations, faith needs to forge new languages, starting with awareness
of the culture, and going on to develop a capacity to 'think' and
choose, to find the support of community, and most of all, to create
a spirituality for living the gospel 'in' but not 'of' today's 'world'.

A recognition of the radically different culture that surrounds
us today has been a constant theme in the various chapters of this
book. It is also implied by the oft-repeated call by Pope John Paul
II for a 'new evangelisation', which he sees as responding to the
new secular mood of culture, a situation requiring new depth and
maturity of faith in people today. Hence evangelisation has to be
'new in its urgency, in its methods, and in its expression'.[4]

Seamus Heaney's poem records an old world filled with sacra-
mentality, but the enormous changes in culture have made that
sensibility unreachable and unreal for many people today. Different
roads need to be travelled towards the option of faith. What used
to be a natural inheritance – a sense of the Christian sacred – has
now to be built afresh, overcoming many desacralising influences.
And yet it is vital that reconstruction of faith be tackled not in a
spirit of nostalgia or return to the past, nor in a spirit of hostility
or resentment of the present. Since the call of God's Spirit is creative
in the now of each culture, we need to read the situation with a
trust that it too can become fertile ground for new languages of
faith.

A frequent theme in our previous chapters has been the sense
of fragmentation induced by contemporary culture. Both modernity and postmodernity can leave us spiritually confused and
adrift, as Heaney's poem evokes. We have also noted the emergence of cultural tendencies that counter this negative inheritance.
Many people are conscious of having lost something precious in
the process of our Western development. Hence one hears of

attempts at retrieval of spaces for the spirit. In fact the need for such cultural recovery was a spur for J. R. R. Tolkien's writing of his famous *Lord of the Rings*. In his view we had neglected the springs of wonder in our pursuit of surface living, and therefore he saw his writing of fantasy as a way to refresh our imagination and to put it in contact again with larger hopes. In his own words, a fairy story can let us experience 'a sudden and miraculous grace', that 'lets a gleam come through' and so 'we see in a brief vision that the answer may be greater'.[5] The very success of his work, as fiction and now as film, shows that it meets a real hunger in people. Even though it is not explicitly religious or Christian, Tolkien's inspiration was firmly and consciously rooted in the gospel. He wanted to awaken the adventure of redemption in human imagination for a culture where that language of desire seemed faded or forgotten. In other words his creative writings sought to make spiritual journeys real again for people. In this direction his work is not alone: as this chapter will explore, there is an exciting new awareness, in recent times and in many quarters, that our culture needs to rediscover spiritual roots in order to survive.

Meanings of spirituality today

The word 'spirituality' needs some initial comment, because its significance has changed hugely in recent years and it is in danger of becoming both vogue-ish and vague. Until the sixties, at least in Catholic circles, it was largely identified with the 'inner life', with individual prayer, and often with some tradition of a religious order (Benedictine, Jesuit, Carmelite etc.). Now it has become a 'buzz-word' even outside church circles. As against the frequent association of old-style spirituality with asceticism (self-renunciation and the pursuit of perfection), contemporary spirituality prefers to be 'life-expanding' and incarnational, liberating a flow of divine energy in each person, and staying more in touch with the struggles of history.[6]

The older spiritualities were vertical roads of questing for God beyond this world. The newer ones stress a this-worldly fullness of life, as an experience of Christian faith. Influenced by the surrounding culture, with its hope for authenticity in the ordinary, do these more 'life-centred' approaches to spirituality reflect the 'eclipse of the transcendent'? Or, in their search for a more holistic living of faith, can this contemporary sensibility construct a new 'range of spirituality' different 'from any other time in human history'?[7] It is clear that the spiritual gateway into faith is central for many people today, and indeed without a reimagined spirituality Christianity is fated to become a museum piece for many in the younger generations.

Sandra Schneiders offers an account of spirituality which remains open to Christian or secular interpretations: 'the experience of consciously striving to integrate one's life in terms not of isolation and self-absorption but of self-transcendence toward the ultimate value one perceives'.[8] In fact in today's culture many humanistic versions of spirituality abound, stressing openness and connectedness. Spirituality is a zone of convergence where theology, prayer and commitments come together as a 'conscious human response to God'.[9] For Christians, spirituality is the way we breathe our Spirit-given freedom in the changing situations of our lives. It is not simply the 'inner life': no phrase like that was ever on the lips of Jesus.

However, a specifically Christian sense of spirituality seems under threat today from enticing but ultimately deceptive forms of inner searching. How are we to discern these cultural currents? The human desire underlying any spiritual quest is very simple: we want more than the merely visible. Humanistic forms of spirituality focus on our potential for life-expansion through inner attentiveness. They offer various approaches to integrating our journeys of self-transcendence. They can be accused of remaining 'therapeutic' and of measuring everything by the peace one feels within. A recent popular book, which is not explicitly Christian, insists that spirituality need not mean breaking loose from gravity into some special enlightenment: 'The contemporary trend to view spirituality as something sweet disguises its power and persuades people to take it too lightly . . . Spirituality doesn't grow like a flower; rather it comes into being like a temple . . . through hard work, imagination and skill.'[10]

This is both attractive and honest, even if it is shy about the gift of relationship that is the core of Christian spirituality. A specifically Christian approach need not exclude wavelengths of deep searching that come from humanistic or non-Christian spiritual traditions: there is a convergence between all forms of authentic expansion of heart and vision. But it will be rooted in 'lived Christian faith' (Sandra Schneiders again), in those practices in which the mystery of Christ is experienced prayerfully and appropriated gradually in people's lives.

In particular a Christian spirituality will be uniquely shaped by four central Christian mysteries.

1.   It will be a relationship with God, rooted in the firstness of God's love for us and in a sense of the Trinity, not as a distant doctrine, but as God's own mutuality in giving and receiving.

2.   It will be an incarnate adventure in the realities of life, inspired and accompanied by the person of Jesus Christ.

3.   It will have the courage to face ordeals and tragedies, trusting in the 'law of the Cross' (Lonergan), the love-triumph we glimpse in Christ's death and resurrection.

4.   It will be marked by care for the wounded of the world and by forgiveness of others, because Christ does not exist really for us, says Jon Sobrino of El Salvador, unless he challenges us to an alternative way of living.

Those four notes draw on the core content of Christian revelation. But these hopes need grounding in formative practices and in this sense Christian spirituality seems to have three main thrusts today.

1.   It highlights the *lived experience* of faith, giving more attention to faith-response to God rather than to doctrine.

2.   It is *developmental* in the sense of fostering growth in contemplative and committed love.

3.   It teaches *practical* skills to nourish a conscious relationship with God through prayer and other reflective exercises.

Understood in this way, Christian spirituality has to do with building daily bridges between the gift of God in Christ and the limited realities of each one's life-situation. As such it is the essential link between faith and culture in most people's lives. It is the zone where they opt to give attention or not to the calls of the Spirit, where they shape the quality of their Christian journey, where they protect the freedom of their hearts, and where they learn to discern wisely amid the pressures of the culture. Adapting Socrates, the undiscerned and unlistening life is not worth living – especially so since we no longer live in pre-modernity and culture no longer carries us towards Christian faith. Either we drift confusedly in the culture around or we seize the rudder of spirituality to steer our course in harmony with the gospel.

Thus spirituality is a practical human art, for a more than human adventure. It starts from beyond us in God's desire to relate (amazingly) to us and to open the Trinity-communion to us. In practice this means being led beyond ourselves into a slow erosion of egoism and a long learning of love. It entails a drama of receiving in order to give, one that echoes the story of revelation itself. In this sense it is never simply the 'inner life': rather it is a whole way of wisdom where we grasp the gift of our freedom in Christ. And whenever that freedom and that gift are imperilled by the culture, spirituality can provide skills of self-defence.

The need for spiritual shields

Perhaps the greatest danger to our humanity within today's culture lies in being disconnected from our depths. Within each person is a whole cluster of capacities of the heart – for wonder, searching, listening, receptivity, and life options for compassion and love. These are spiritual dimensions in everyone and they constitute the basis for the hearing from which faith is born. But one by-product of the fragmentations and pressures of today is that this whole zone can remain underdeveloped. It is one form of the cultural malnutrition (or cultural desolation, as discussed earlier). In the language of the parable of the Sower, culture can become a multi-faceted enemy for faith – robbing the seed, making shallow the roots, or choking the fragile plant.

When whole cultures remain 'trapped at the surface level', alien-ated from the deepest languages of our humanity, then 'reconnection with depth is the central issue'.[11] In older argumentation about faith one spoke about intellectual 'preambles' for belief in God. Now those preambles have to be spiritual, cultural and artistic – in order to prepare the receiving apparatus for faith by reopening contact points with human depth. We need rescuing from the surfaces where a certain kind of dominant culture can trap our spiritual sensibilities. How can this come about? Only through experiences that reach and liberate the imagination and the heart. Without 'preambles of disposition', to nourish wonder and invite into deeper levels of listening, the whole effort to make sense of God can be handicapped from the outset.[12] This is a task for poetry in the largest sense – not necessarily written poetry in verse, but various forms of imaginative communication that awaken the slumbering sense of mystery and of longing for something more. It is in this spirit that Vaclav Havel, while insisting on his own religious uncertainty, has quoted Heidegger's saying that 'only a God can save us now', and goes on to speak of today's multicultural world as needing to be 'rooted in self-transcendence'. Merely technological responses will not meet the hungers of our culture, because 'we are in a different place and facing a different situation' where the false confidence of modernity has to give way to 'something deeper'.[13]

The road of depth is certainly one of the avenues of hope for culture today, and for its religious renewal. But this emphasis on its own will not prove sufficient; indeed it can turn out to be a narcissistic turning inwards, a depth without contact with the calls of history or with the surprise of revelation. When 'uncoupled' from the cost and concreteness of the Bible, spirituality can serve merely 'therapeutic and self-expressive goals'.[14] In every age of culture, however, Christian faith has proved an extraordinary source of depth – through contemplative wisdom, or artistic creativity, or intellectual synthesis, or social vision. But this depth always saw itself as secondary to the gift of God in the event of Christ. Christian interiority can never be content with mere withdrawal and serenity, because the cry of tragedy and injustice and the reminders of the prophets challenge that depth to do something about this wounded world, and to do so in God's name and in imitation of Christ. A renewal of depth is a crucial strand in the healing of our cultural impoverishments, but it is not the entire Christian response to culture.

Tensions in theology

It is not surprising to find that the tensions arising over the spirituality needed for contemporary culture find their parallels in theological polarities of today. Putting it very simply, there are at least three competing models of theology – liberation, dialogue and revelation. For the liberationist, faith has to shows itself in works, in praxis, in transformative commitment within the many justice battlegrounds of history; otherwise it is in danger of being unfaithful to the prophetic call at the heart of the Bible and the contemporary cry of pain from the majority of people on our planet. Hence the approach to culture is one of critique, of aggressive discernment and of seeking to construct alternative communities of solidarity to counter the structural evils of today.

According to the dialogue model, we need to start from 'below', paying attention to the tone of human searching today. Theology needs to listen to the culture in its depth and even in its surfaces. Otherwise we risk unreality and irrelevance. To ignore the human hearer is insensitivity to the incarnation. This stress on dialogue calls for contact in the first place but also for discernment, both positive and negative, trusting that we can discover signposts of the Spirit within contemporary hungers and questions.

For the revelation model, God has spoken 'from above', once and for all in Christ. All else is relative beside this Word as gift and judgement. Where the dialogue approach finds mediations of grace in the human, the revelationist stresses the disruptive beauty of God's wisdom and the fallacy of any anthropological yardsticks from the point of view of faith. All culture remains flawed and secondary because it is a human construct. Where the liberationist tends to interpret culture as structures in need of conversion, the revelationist views culture as the ground within which the seed has to be sown and a more transcendent Kingdom proclaimed. In brief, the liberation school offers a radical critique of culture as embodying assumptions of irresponsible escapism. The dialogue model prefers instead to listen for the deeper desires of the culture in its various levels. The revelation approach wants to recreate culture into Christian forms, to convert human attitudes to the unique light of the gospel.

In recent years, at least within Catholicism, there has been an unfortunate tendency to ideologise and polarise these stances. It is strange to run into those who will read and follow only von Balthasar or only Rahner or only Gutiérrez, and see the positions of others as almost heretical. However, if we shift the wavelength from ideas to spirituality, what seem like incompatible divergences can be found to converge into a potentially important unity. There are undoubtedly major divergences between these theologians; confronted, however, with the acute pastoral crisis of our culture, they discover a new harmony, where each emphasis is essential for modelling an alternative Christian culture to rival the dominant imagination.

James Bacik speaks of a 'postmodern spirituality which is more attuned to the mystery dimension of life', and he lists some of its possible characteristics.[15] As against the individualistic and rationalist approaches fostered by modernity, the postmodern moment calls forth different tones: 'more communal, intuitive and reflective'; 'explicitly relational'; pluralistic, combining 'acceptance and protest', as well as the mystical and the prophetic dimensions of faith. Independently I had prepared the following diagram that echoes much the same line of thought. It is intended to show how some principal features of the postmodern sensibility awaken ancient dimensions of Christian faith.

Postmodern sensibility	*Notes within faith*
1. Distrust of rationalism	Narrative and negative theology
2. Awareness of the feminine and the ecological	Christian connectedness/ holism
3. Quest for post-materialist quality of life	Gospel as an alternative 'Way'
4. Return of affectivity	Contemplative skills of prayer
5. Sense of dispersal	Community as support
6. Disillusion with utopias	Compassion and social solidarity

1. Down through the ages faith has always had to insist that while it is reasonable, it goes beyond the merely rationalist because it depends on God's revelation; theology today is recovering an appreciation of its roots in story and in beauty, as well as a sense of its darkness as a mystery beyond the excessive clarity of words and concepts.

2. From its understanding of creation and incarnation, Christian faith has a special reverence for the material world and for humanity as its crown. Those aspects of spirituality were somewhat neglected in recent centuries but are now re-emerging under the impetus of secular developments; faith can find inspiration from cultural sensibilities born outside the Church (as acknowledged in *Gaudium et Spes*, No. 44).

3. Ronald Rolheiser speaks of the emergence in today's culture of a new 'non-contemplative personality' with a shrunken capacity for wonder and for inner awareness.[16] Faith always meant a conversion of heart through accepting the gospel; today, faced with the often shallow way of life promoted by the dominant culture, we realise more dramatically that Christian faith is a radically different 'Way' (that word being one of the New Testament terms for living out one's yes to Christ).

The final three constitute the essential pillars of faith in every age: from the Acts of the Apostles onwards Christianity fostered (4) worship, (5) belonging and (6) active service of those in need. Similarly, Christian spirituality for today's culture needs a triple initiation – of contemplative depth, of experience of community, and of lived options of self-giving.

4. The Italian theologian Pierangelo Sequeri has explored the retrieval of feelings in contemporary culture, arguing that against the deadening rhythms of urban life today people are aware of two human zones they can trust: individual emotion and the feeling of love.[17] In his view, however, these precious areas are also in danger of trivial interpretations unless transformed by the costly love at the heart of the gospel. Where people learn to pray personally they are escaping from that narrow prison of utilitarian living, precisely

through encountering what is at the heart of the revelationist's concern: the uniqueness of Christ.

5.   The paradox of the 'lonely crowd' is still a reality for contemporary cultures. When people discover the slow journey of dialogue with others, and when they learn through that companionship and searching, they are echoing the hopes of the dialogue model.

6.   Whenever they learn through contact with the pain of others that they have a generosity within them that the world needs, and if they choose to commit themselves in some concrete road of service or struggle, then they are in touch with what liberation spirituality calls conversion through praxis.

A convergence to meet a convergence

Martin Buber once commented that the real danger of Egypt was that the Israelites would come to think of the situation there as normal. Our temptation is to think of the culture that kidnaps the imagination, rendering faith unreachable for many, as somehow beyond question: it's the way things are. But there are wiser responses to the omnipresent and omni-shaping culture than a shrug of the shoulders or merely a turning of the back, a locking of Christian doors in defensiveness. This book has suggested analysis, discernment, critique and cultural creation as essential notes in the chord of faith today. Throughout these pages it has been seen how complex a presence culture is, how it involves a convergence of influences that reach us all on the level of the imagination. Not all those influences are malign but many are trivialising, confusing or ambiguous. Only a Christian convergence of strengths can counter this convergence of cultural impoverishments. And the Christian answer has to meet its opponent on the level of experience, imagination and spirituality.

In an interview towards the end of his life, Hans Urs von Balthasar commented that Christians should not distrust modern culture, *provided* 'adequate spiritual discernment is exercised'. He acknowledged that contemporary lifestyles can have a 'seductive influence' on young people but instead of merely moaning about these dangers, he insisted that faith seek to create culture: Christians should commit themselves 'to the whole of secular culture', building 'islands of humanity' in order to 'humanize whatever is threatening to slide into the inhuman'.[18]

To repeat and conclude: there are three converging strengths to be learned – skills of interiority, supports of community, and commitment to service of the wounded of the world. They constitute a pastoral triangle as old as the Acts of the Apostles but as fresh as any alert Christian community today. Where any one of these growth languages is alive and well, there is hope for faith in spite of the complexity of the culture. Where all three flourish, we are well on the way to recreating a living Christian culture for our time.

A Personal Epilogue

Roots and Horizons

You must wait for the eye of the soul to be formed in you. Religious truth is reached, not by reasoning, but by an inward perception. (John Henry Newman)[1]

There's life and there's opera, and I want both. (Mary Oliver)[2]

I had not planned to write this section but I want to end with something simpler and more personal. This book has been complex and theoretical at times. Yet culture is also simple: it is a core vision that each of us has received and that has changed with the years. So, what does it all mean for me? What is my 'culture'? What cultures have formed me? How is it different for the new generation? Answering those questions fully might require an autobiography. But some random reflections may serve as a conclusion and invite the reader to ponder her or his story of this strange reality called culture.

Some years ago I revisited the village of my childhood – Collooney, Co. Sligo, in the North West of Ireland. I was touring with Italian friends and they were interested in seeing where I had grown up. With them I went into the 'sitting room' of the house where I spent my first fifteen years and bought a bar of chocolate! That part of the house had become a small supermarket. The owners were strangers to me; in fact I have no relations in the village any more. Later we met people that I knew, who gave me a warm welcome 'home'; but I realised that only a certain age group had any idea of who I was. With the Italians I walked down the one main street of the village, where I could remember every house and who lived there in the forties and fifties. We went into the church were I had been an altar server for years. Everything seemed vivid like yesterday except that yesterday seemed another world.

This village *was* my culture. 'We were as Danes in Denmark all day long': a line from Wallace Stevens sums it up – a small and total world, which moulded how I feel and imagine everything, even today. Or to quote Yeats (himself from Sligo), a certain 'unity of culture' was strong in my formative years. Since then I have had to learn to move in more complex worlds. Even the fact of walking through Collooney speaking Italian symbolised how horizons had changed. In the small schoolroom, with its turf fire that the rain used to put out, we had studied the geography of Europe (in Gaelic). Now I have been to places I never noticed on the rotating globe on the windowsill: India, Venezuela, Paraguay, Ethiopia, Kenya, Australia, New Zealand, Japan, Iran, Thailand, Malaysia. That village and that family sitting room shaped my roots – and they remain steady – but it is no longer my horizon of culture. On the spot where we listened to the old 'wireless' a cash register now stands. The school itself is a shed for cattle.

Let me switch scene. I have been living in Rome for over ten years now. Sometimes as I walk to the university, to teach theology, I watch the faces in the streets. Since I am often on my way to some class about faith, I find myself wondering about the religious roots, or lack of them, in the young people around me. I become aware of a whole range of nourishment – of the spirit and the imagination – that my childhood gave me; but these young Romans have had little opportunity of this kind. I imagine them, rightly or wrongly, as spiritually lonely: where do they have real community beyond the small circles of friendship? I sense them drifting on the surface of themselves: where do they have languages of wonder that might open towards God? I feel that they have much to give but few channels for giving. They seem more like victims of this moment in history than lost in deliberate laziness or egoism. I picture them as uncalled, unawoken, unreached by the Truth that for me is at the centre of life. What is missing? That unity of culture that Collooney gave me, except that for them it would have to be chosen and created – because their more broken context leaves them (and me in ways) more stranded from reality, from our true humanity, from God. Are my Roman musings too pessimistic? A bit like St Paul in his first reaction to Athens? If so, I need to wait, like him, until I can glimpse the signs of searching beyond the appearances.

Certainly the village world is gone. Mourning its passing is a waste of time. The cities that we 'bought' into (and the word is right) have given us exciting freedoms but many confusions. The contrast with my childhood seems clear. Without idealising or exaggerating (I hope), that village world gave me roots that have been a constant, if often unconscious, blessing. They have been like an anchor that allowed leeway for movement, freedom for change, for other languages in every sense. Where will the children of the city find anchors and roots? In family experience which is the core stability in spite of cultural change?[3] In encountering the stories and symbols of God through the Church? What experiences and images could liberate their hope and incarnate the gospel for them?

Broadening the picture, is our whole culture in flight, not just from roots, but from the cost of conversion? The recurrent tragedies of war or famine, together with the stagnant injustice of our divided worlds, show that something is sick in how we manage this planet. We seem to remain paralysed behind the walls our cultural egoism has constructed. Impotence of imagination rules. Distortions of truth come to seem normal. In the light of faith the conclusion is unoriginal but challenging: Christianity has to enter this battle zone of clashing symbols, in the spirit of a servant, so that redemptive love can undermine the 'imperial' images of an inhuman culture.[4] Bernard Lonergan once wondered whether a culture can recover from decline: 'To my mind the only solution is religious . . . when reasoning is ineffective, what is left but faith', the faith that has as its core a human and divine image of 'self-sacrificing love'.[5] Thus the healing of our ills lies in discovering love through God, or God through love – two seemingly different journeys that in fact converge and give a special tone to being a Christian within today's culture.

Let me evoke two other real experiences: together with some relations I visited the National Gallery in Dublin. We were a group of three adults and five children (aged seven to thirteen). The problem of how not to bore the children solved itself in the best postmodern way! We left them in the new computer section of the gallery, where they happily explored the world of art, fingering the screens of monitors and listening on earphones – allowing the adults to see the real paintings in peace. On our return the children hardly wanted to leave the computers; it was marvellous to watch their ease with technology. It recalls a more recent episode while visiting an Italian family. When a nine-year-old boy invited me to join him in a Play Station game, I killed two people on my side before being quickly eliminated myself. I can find and download theological articles from the Internet but this was a different skill, indeed a different world. Will those children in the gallery ever want to see the real pictures? Are the Play Station children on the threshold of a major cultural shift?

Obviously the roots of many of those growing up in the new culture are shakier than before. Their world is more unsettled and on the move, yet their hungers are real: they want, often shyly or secretly, to find meaning and light. I have spent hundreds of hours listening to young voices in search, sometimes lost in painful fog, sometimes full of energy. And it has been a joyful adventure. In my innocence, however, I sometimes thought that the fruits of a liberating conversation would be enough. I witnessed many people get in touch with themselves and sometimes with the Lord. But the context was too personal. Even if they discovered 'hidden treasure', they went back into what the gospel calls the 'world', to a powerful culture that could easily eclipse their vision and stunt their hope. They needed new spaces with others where they could deepen and live out the challenges of the faith-freedom they had glimpsed. John Paul II was right: a faith that does not find cultural expression will remain immature. When the problem is cultural, the response has to be communal, not just personal.

Returning to the contrast between my childhood and that of the young today, culture seems a dialogue between roots and horizons. The roots come early in life; the novelist Mauriac claimed that the doors of imagination close at twenty. But then comes the longer road of changing horizons. Faith can best flourish and 'become culture' by entering that drama – watering the roots of imagination, offering shared spaces of nourishment and call, and embracing with Spirit-courage the adventure of cultural change.

Appendix

Anthology of Quotations

The extracts are in chronological order

It is one of the marks of the human person to reach true and authentic humanity only through culture, that is, by cultivating natural gifts and values. Whenever human life is involved, nature and culture are intimately connected.

In its general sense the word 'culture' stands for everything by which human beings refine and develop their various capacities of mind and body. It includes efforts to control the cosmos by knowledge or by work, as well as ways of humanizing social life within the family or civic community through the progress of customs and institutions.

(Second Vatican Council, *Gaudium et Spes*, 1965, no. 53)

A theology mediates between a cultural matrix and the significance and role of a religion in that matrix. The classicist notion of culture was normative: at least *de jure* there was but one culture that was both universal and permanent; to its norms and ideals might aspire the uncultured, whether they were the young or the people or the natives or the barbarians. Besides the classicist, there also is the empirical notion of culture. It is the set of meanings and values that informs a way of life. It may remain unchanged for ages. It may be in process of slow development or rapid dissolution.

(Bernard Lonergan, *Method in Theology*, Darton, Longman & Todd, London, 1972, p. xi)

The Church is an evangelizer, but it begins by being evangelized itself ... if it wants to retain freshness, vigour, and strength in order to proclaim the Gospel ...

What matters is to evangelize human culture and cultures (not in a purely decorative way as it were by applying a thin veneer, but in a vital way, in depth and right to their very roots) ... always taking the person as one's starting point and always coming back to the relationship of people among themselves and with God.

The Gospel, and therefore evangelization, are certainly not identical with culture, and they are independent in regard to all cultures. Nevertheless, the Kingdom which the Gospel proclaims is lived by people who are profoundly linked to a culture, and the building up of the Kingdom cannot avoid borrowing the elements of human culture or cultures. Though independent of cultures, the Gospel and evangelization are not necessarily incompatible with them; rather they are capable of permeating them all without becoming subject to any one of them.

The split between the Gospel and culture is without doubt the drama of our time, just as it was of other times. Therefore every effort must be made to ensure a full evangelization of culture, or more correctly of cultures.

(Paul VI, *Evangelii nuntiandi*, 1975, §§ 15, 20)

[Culture] means simply the patterned way in which people do things together ... Culture implies a measure of homogeneity ... Culture holds people together over a span of time. It is received from the past, but not by any process of natural inheritance. It has to be learned afresh by each generation ... Culture covers everything in human life. At its centre is a world-view, that is, a general understanding of the nature of the universe and of one's place in it ... From this basic world-view flow both standards of judgement or values and standards of conduct ... Cultures are never static; there is a continuous process of change ...

[In synthesis] Culture is an integrated system of beliefs (about God or reality or ultimate meaning), of values (about what is true, good, beautiful and normative), of customs (how to behave, relate to others, talk, pray, dress, work, play, trade, farm, eat, etc.) and of institutions which express those beliefs, values and customs ... which bind a society together and gives it a sense of identity, dignity, security, and continuity.

(From the Willowbank Report, Lausanne Committee for World Evangelization, 1978)

I stress the necessity of mobilizing all sources which direct the spiritual dimension of human existence, and which bear witness to the primacy of the spiritual inhumanity – and which corresponds to the dignity of intelligence, will and heart – in order not to succumb again to the monstrous alienation of collective evil ... (4)

Thanks to culture a person lives a really human life. Human life is culture in this sense too that, through it, human beings are distinguished and differentiated from everything that exists in the visible world: human beings cannot do without culture ... In the unity of culture as the specific way of human existence, there is rooted at the same time the plurality of cultures within which people live. In this plurality, a person develops without losing, however, the essential contact with the unity of culture as the fundamental and essential dimension of one's existence and being. (6)

The human being who, in the visible world, in the only ontic subject of culture, is also its only object and its term. Culture is that through which the human being, as human, becomes more human, 'is' more, has more access to 'being' ... People think of culture and speak about it in the first place in relation to the nature of the human being, then only in a secondary and indirect way in relation to the world of human products ... A human being, and only a human being, is the 'protagonist' or 'architect' of culture ... (7)

Human cultures reflect, there is no doubt, the various systems of production relations; however, it is not such and such a system that is at the origin of culture, but human beings, who live in the system, who accept it or try to change it. A culture without human subjectivity and without human causality is inconceivable; in the cultural field, the human being is always the first fact – the prime and fundamental fact of culture. And one is so, always, in one's totality: in one's spiritual and material subjectivity as a complete whole ... (8)

[There exists a] fundamental link between the Gospel, that is, the message of Christ and the Church, and a human being in one's very humanity. This link is in fact a creator of culture in its very foundation. To create culture, it is necessary to consider, to its last consequences and entirely, the human being as a particular and autonomous value, as the subject bearing the transcendency of the person. Human beings must be affirmed for themselves, and not for any other motive or reason: solely for themselves! (10)

The future of humanity depends on culture. (23)

John Paul II, UNESCO, Paris, 2 June 1980)

Culture may now be said to be the whole complex of distinctive features, spiritual, material, intellectual and emotional, that characterize a society or social group. It includes not only the arts and letters, but also modes of life, the fundamental rights of human being, value systems, traditions and beliefs . . . It is culture that gives the ability to reflect. It is culture that makes us specifically human, rational beings, endowed with critical judgement and a sense of moral commitment. It is through culture that we discern values and make choices. It is through culture that human beings express themselves, become aware of themselves, recognize their incompleteness, question their own achievements, seek untiringly for new meanings and create works through which they transcend their limitations.

(UNESCO definition, Mexico conference, 1982)

Culture is the expression of the identity of a human community. Culture refers to the delicate fabric of habits, symbols, artistic representations, tools, rules of behaviour, moral values and institutions through which the human community orders its relationships to nature, to other communities and to reality as a whole. Through processes of socialisation and through tradition, a culture is being transmitted to the following generations. In this sense, culture is specifically human; it is the second 'nature' of human beings in their social relationships. Any understanding of culture includes the language, history, family patterns, etc. of a given community.

(Konrad Raiser, Secretary General, WCC, 1994)

Notes

Introduction: Culture as Cinderella

1. T. S. Eliot, *Notes towards the Definition of Culture* (Faber & Faber, London, 1948), p. 27.
2. William Lynch, *Christ and Prometheus* (University of Notre Dame Press, Notre Dame, 1970), p. 28.
3. Samuel Huntington, 'The clash of civilizations?', *Foreign Affairs* (Summer 1993), 22–49. Quotations from pp. 22, 31.
4. Nicholas Boyle, *Who Are We Now? Christian humanism and the global market from Hegel to Heaney* (T. & T. Clark, Edinburgh, 1998), p. 9.
5. Anthony D. Smith, *National Identity* (Penguin Books, London, 1991), pp. 155, 159.
6. Thomas L. Friedman, *The Lexus and the Olive Tree* (Anchor Books, New York, 2000), p. 232.
7. Konrad Raiser, *For a Culture of Life: transforming globalization and violence* (WCC Publications, Geneva, 2002), p. 26.
8. Fred Inglis, *Cultural Studies* (Blackwell, Oxford, 1993), pp. xi, 247.
9. Stephen L. Carter, *The Culture of Disbelief: how American law and politics trivialize religious devotion* (Basic Books, New York, 1993), pp. 22, 25, 44.
10. Bernard Lonergan, *Method in Theology* (Darton, Longman & Todd, London, 1972), p. xi.
11. Bernard Lonergan, *Collection*, ed. F. E. Crowe (Darton, Longman & Todd, London, 1967), p. 266.
12. Aylward Shorter, *Towards a Theology of Inculturation* (Geoffrey Chapman, London, 1988), p. 4.
13. This phrase is from Raymond Williams, *The Long Revolution* (Chatto & Windus, London, 1961), p. 48.
14. Edward T. Hall, *Beyond Culture* (Anchor Books, New York, 1977), p. 85.
15. Bernard Ostry, *The Cultural Connection* (McClelland and Stewart, Toronto, 1978), p. 1. Used by permission of the author.
16. Immanuel Wallerstein, *Geopolitics and Geoculture: essays on the changing world-system* (Cambridge University Press, Cambridge, 1991), pp. 182–3.

Chapter 1: *Clarifying the Concept*

1. Terry Eagleton, *The Idea of Culture* (Blackwell, Oxford, 2000), p. 131.
2. Marilyn J. Legge, 'Bricoleurs-in-community: reframing theologies of culture', *Religious Studies and Theology* (Vol. 16, 1997), 12.
3. Matthew Arnold, *Culture and Anarchy*, ed. R. H. Super (University of Michigan Press, Ann Arbor, 1965), pp. 95, 112.
4. Edward B. Tylor, *Primitive Culture* (John Murray, London, 1871), Vol. 1, p. 1.
5. Roger Scruton, *An Intelligent Person's Guide to Modern Culture* (Duckworth, London, 1998), p. 2.
6. Quoted in Lawrence Osborn, *Restoring the Vision: the gospel and modern culture* (Mowbray, London, 1995), p. 1.
7. Kathryn Tanner, *Theories of Culture: a new agenda for theology* (Fortress Press, Minneapolis, 1997), p. 26.
8. Lieven Boeve, 'Market and religion in postmodern culture', *Theology* (Vol. 102, 1999), 29.
9. A. L. Kroeber and Clyde Kluckhohn, *Culture: a critical review of concepts and definitions* (Vintage Books, New York, 1963).
10. *ibid.*, p. 128.
11. Clifford Geertz, *The Interpretation of Cultures* (Basic Books, New York, 1973), p. 89.
12. *ibid.*, p. 5.
13. Robert J. Schreiter, *Constructing Local Theologies* (SCM Press, London, 1985), p. 55.
14. Geertz, *op.cit.*, pp. 17, 28.
15. Geertz, *op.cit.*, p. 44.
16. Geertz, *op.cit.*, p. 46.
17. Bradd Shore, *Culture in Mind: cognition, culture and the problem of meaning* (Oxford University Press, New York, 1996), p. 51.
18. Clifford Geertz, *Local Knowledge: further essays in interpretive anthropology* (Basic Books, New York, 1983), p. 85.
19. *ibid.*, p. 75.
20. Ann Swidler, 1986 article quoted in James Côté and Charles Levine, *Identity Formation, Agency, and Culture* (Lawrence Erlbaum, Mahwah, 2002), p. 122. See also Ann Swidler, *Talk of Love: how culture matters* (University of Chicago Press, Chicago, 2001).
21. Bernard Lonergan, *Insight: a study of human understanding* (Longman, London, 1957), p. 236.
22. Bernard Lonergan, *Method in Theology* (Darton, Longman & Todd, London, 1972), p. 301.
23. *ibid.*, p. 57.
24. Bernard Lonergan, *A Second Collection* (Darton, Longman & Todd, London, 1974), p. 91.
25. *ibid.*, p. 92.

26. Lonergan, *Method*, p. 363.
27. Raymond Williams, *The Long Revolution* (Chatto & Windus, London, 1961), p. 41.
28. *ibid.*, pp. 48, 72.
29. Raymond Williams, *Culture and Society* (Hogarth Press, London, 1993), 1958 Introduction, p. xvi.
30. Raymond Williams, 'Culture is ordinary', reprinted in *Studying Culture: an introductory reader*, ed. Ann Gray and Jim McGuigan (Edward Arnold, London, 1993), pp. 5–14. Quotation from p. 6.
31. Raymond Williams, *Culture* (Fontana, London, 1981), pp. 10–12.
32. Williams, *Culture and Society*, p. 325.
33. Williams, *Culture*, p. 209.
34. *ibid.*, p. 13.
35. *ibid.*, p. 206.
36. Pierre Bourdieu et al., *Academic Discourse* (Polity Press, Cambridge, 1994), p. 8; Bourdieu, *Algeria 1960: the disenchantment of the world* (Cambridge, Cambridge University Press, 1979), p. vii.
37. As quoted by Hervé Carrier in *The Church and Culture since Vatican II*, ed. Joseph Gremillion (University of Notre Dame Press, Notre Dame, 1985), p. 19.
38. See Charles R. Taber, *The World Is Too Much With Us: 'culture' in modern Protestant missions* (Mercer University Press, Macon, 1991), p. 5.

Chapter 2: Four Theorists of Change

1. Mary Douglas, 'The effects of modernization on religious change' in *Religion and America: spiritual life in a secular age*, ed. M. Douglas and S. Tipton (Beacon Press, Boston, 1983), p. 26.
2. Walter J. Ong, *Frontiers in American Catholicism* (Macmillan, New York, 1961), p. 102.
3. Mary Douglas, *Natural Symbols: explorations in cosmology* (Cresset Press, London, 1970), p. x.
4. *ibid.*, p. ix.
5. Mary Douglas, *In the Wilderness* (Academic Press, Sheffield, 1993), p. 47.
6. Mary Douglas, *Risk and Blame: essays in cultural theory* (Routledge, London, 1992), p. 125.
7. See Gerald A. Arbuckle, *Refounding the Church* (Geoffrey Chapman, London, 1993), p. 81.
8. Douglas, *Natural Symbols*, p. 60.
9. Douglas, *In the Wilderness*, pp. 45, 47.
10. *ibid*, p. 4.
11. Arbuckle, *op. cit.*, p. 88.

12. Douglas, *In the Wilderness*, p. 44.

13. Douglas, *Risk and Blame*, pp. 136–7.

14. Margaret Archer, *Culture and Agency: the place of culture in social theory* (Cambridge University Press, Cambridge, 1988), pp. xv, xxii.

15. *ibid.*, pp. 12, 18.

16. *ibid.*, p. xv.

17. Walter J Ong, *Orality and Literacy: the technologizing of the word* (Routledge, London, 1982), pp. 78, 178–9.

18. Walter J. Ong, *The Presence of the Word: some prolegomena for culture and religious history* (Simon & Schuster, New York, 1970), pp. 111, 117.

19. *ibid.*, p. 125. See also Walter J. Ong, *Ramus, Method, and the Decay of Dialogue* (Harvard University Press, Cambridge, 1958).

20. Walter J. Ong, *Interfaces of the Word: studies in the evolution of consciousness and culture* (Cornell University Press, Ithaca, 1977), p. 222.

21. Walter J. Ong, *Faith and Contexts* [Collected Essays 1952–91], 2 vols., ed. Thomas Farrell (Scholars Press, Atlanta, 1992), vol. II, p. 162.

22. René Girard, *I See Satan Fall Like Lightning* (Orbis Books, New York, 2001), p. 83.

23. René Girard, *Things Hidden since the Foundation of the World* (Athlone Press, London, 1987), p. 26.

24. Michel de Certeau, *Culture in the Plural* (University of Minnesota Press, Minneapolis, 1998).

25. *The Girard Reader*, ed. James Williams (Crossroad, New York, 1997), p. 262.

26. Girard, *Things Hidden*, pp. 430–1.

27. James Alison, *The Joy of Being Wrong: original sin through Easter eyes* (Crossroad, New York, 1998), pp. 33, 445, 280.

28. Girard, *I See Satan*, p. 178.

Chapter 3: A Major Theme of Vatican II

1. Quoted by Frederick Crowe in *Bernard Lonergan* (Geoffrey Chapman, London, 1992), p. 98.

2. Dermot Lane (ed.), *Religion and Culture in Dialogue* (Columba Press, Dublin, 1993), p. 14.

3. Quoted in Giovanni Turbanti, *Un concilio per il mondo moderno* (Mulino, Bologna, 2000), p. 106.

Chapter 4: Catholic Developments since 1965

1. Margaret O'Brien Steinfels, 'Beyond assimilation: let's get wise' in *The Catholic Church and American Culture*, ed. Cassian Yuhaus (Paulist Press, New York, 1990), p. 36.
2. Michael Novak, *The Catholic Ethic and the Spirit of Capitalism* (Free Press, New York, 1993), p. 214.
3. Fernando Miguens, *Fe y Culture en la Enseñanza de Juan Pablo II* (Ediciones Palabra, Madrid, 1994).
4. Avery Dulles, 'The prophetic humanism of John Paul II', *America* (23 October 1993), 9.
5. Karol Wojtyla, *Person and Community: selected essays*, tr. Theresa Sandok (Peter Lang, New York, 1993), pp. 265–6.
6. *ibid.*, p. 267.
7. *ibid.*, pp. 269, 271.
8. *ibid.*, pp. 272–3.
9. Miguens, *op. cit.*, pp. 169–70 (my translation).

Chapter 5: The World Council of Churches

1. Quoted in S. Wesley Ariarajah, *Gospel and Culture: an ongoing discussion within the Ecumenical Movement* (Gospel and Cultures Pamphlet 1, WCC Publications, Geneva, 1994), p. 28.
2. 'On intercultural hermeneutics' [Report of a WCC theological consultation, Jerusalem, December 1995], *International Review of Mission* (Vol. 85, No. 337, 1996), 242.
3. C. Duraisingh (ed.), *Called to One Hope: the gospel in diverse cultures*, (WCC Publications, Geneva, 1998).
4. Konrad Raiser, 'Gospel and cultures', *International Review of Mission* (Vol. 83, No. 331, 1994), 623.
5. Emilio Castro, 'On evangelism and culture: some reflections', *International Review of Mission* (Vol. 84, No. 335, 1995), 365–78. References here are to pp. 366–7.
6. Ariarajah, *op. cit.* In the following paragraphs, which summarise this fine essay, page references will be given in parenthesis in the text.
7. *Study Process on Gospel and Cultures* (WCC, Geneva, 1995), p. 6.
8. Christopher Duraisingh, 'Looking towards Salvador: editorial', *International Review of Mission* (Vol. 84, No. 334, 1995), 206.
9. These questions are paraphrased from pp. 6–18 of the Study Process booklet mentioned in note 7.
10. In these paragraphs the abbreviation *COH* will be used to refer to *Called to One Hope* (the book cited in note 3 above).

11. Christopher Duraisingh, 'Authentic witness within each culture: editorial', *International Review of Mission* (Vol. 84, No. 335, 1995), 361–2.

Chapter 6: Incoming Tides of Modernity

1. Jane Collier in *The Gospel and Contemporary Culture*, ed. Hugh Montefiore (Mowbray, London, 1992), p. 112.
2. Stuart Hall, 'The question of cultural identity' in *The Polity Reader in Cultural Theory* (Polity Press, Cambridge, 1994), p. 119.
3. Kieran Flanagan, *Sociology and Liturgy: re-presentations of the holy* (Macmillan, London, 1991), p. 324.
4. Leszek Kolakowski, *Modernity on Endless Trial* (University of Chicago Press, Chicago, 1990), p. 6.
5. Louis Dupré, *Passage to Modernity* (Yale University Press, New Haven, 1993), *passim*.
6. Hannah Arendt, *The Human Condition* (University of Chicago Press, Chicago, 1958), p. 248.
7. *ibid.*, p. 305.
8. Dupré, *op. cit.*, p. 249.
9. *Autonomy and Solidarity: interviews with Jürgen Habermas*, ed. Peter Dews (Verso, London, 1992), pp. 225, 227.
10. Alain Touraine, *Critique of Modernity* (Blackwell, Oxford, 1995), p. 340.
11. *ibid.*, pp. 345, 29.
12. *ibid.*, p. 314.
13. *ibid.*, p. 292.
14. *ibid.*, pp. 322, 318.
15. Charles Taylor, *Sources of the Self: the making of modern identity* (Harvard University Press, Cambridge, 1989), p. 429.
16. *ibid.*, pp. 506–7, 520.
17. Charles Taylor, *The Ethics of Authenticity* (Harvard University Press, Cambridge, 1991), p. 10.
18. *ibid.*, pp. 17–18.
19. *ibid.*, p. 16.
20. *ibid.*, p. 35.
21. *ibid.*, p. 69.
22. *ibid.*, pp. 118, 101.
23. *A Catholic Modernity? Charles Taylor's Marianist Award Lecture*, ed. James Heft (Oxford University Press, New York, 1999), p. 16.
24. *ibid.*, pp. 37, 124.

Chapter 7: Religious Responses to Modernity

1. David Walsh, *The Third Millennium: reflections on faith and reason* (Georgetown University Press, Washington, 1999), p. 111.
2. José Casanova, *Public Religions in the Modern World* (University of Chicago Press, Chicago, 1994), p. 234.
3. *L'Osservatore Romano*, 25 September 1994, p. 5.
4. Casanova, *op. cit.*, pp. 214, 234.
5. See Gilles Langevin, 'L'inculturation selon le magistère de l'Eglise catholique romaine', *Nouveau Dialogue* (Montreal, No. 97, 1993), p. 23.
6. Peter L. Berger (ed.), *The Desecularization of the World: resurgent religion and world politics* (Eerdmans, Grand Rapids, 1999), p. 9.
7. Walsh, *op. cit.*, pp. 18–19.
8. Christopher Dawson, *Religion and Culture* (Sheed & Ward, London, 1948), p. 217.
9. Christopher Dawson, *Understanding Europe* (Sheed & Ward, London, 1952), pp. 241, 244–5.
10. Romano Guardini, *The End of the Modern World* (Sheed & Ward, London, 1950), pp. 52, 56.
11. *ibid.*, p. 61.
12. *ibid.*, pp. 97–8.
13. Romano Guardini, *Letters from Lake Como* (Ressourcement edition, William Eerdmans, Grand Rapids, 1994), pp. 63, 80, 81.
14. Guardini, *The End of the Modern World*, pp. 112–13.
15. Hervé Carrier, *Evangelizing the Culture of Modernity* (Orbis Books, New York, 1993), p. 35.
16. *ibid.*, p. 42.
17. *ibid.*, p. 62.
18. Lesslie Newbigin, *Gospel in a Pluralist Society* (SPCK, London, 1989), pp. 187–9.
19. Quoted in George R. Hunsberger, *Bearing the Witness of the Spirit: Lesslie Newbigin's theology of cultural plurality* (Eerdmans, Grand Rapids, 1998), p. 239.
20. Lesslie Newbegin, *Foolishness to the Greeks* (SPCK, London, 1986), p. 24.
21. *ibid.*, p. 58.
22. Lesslie Newbigin, 'Ecumenical amnesia', *International Bulletin of Missionary Research* (Vol. 18, January 1994), 2–5. Quotations from p. 3.
23. Lawrence Osborn, *Restoring the Vision: the gospel and modern culture* (Mowbray, London, 1995), p. 146.
24. Hugh Montefiore (ed.), *The Gospel and Contemporary Culture* (Mowbray, London, 1992). Quotation from Montefiore's introduction, pp. 4–5.

25. Michael Nazir-Ali, quoted in *The Gospel and Our Culture* (Newsletter, Issue 35, Autumn 2002), p. 1. More information on this movement can be found at www.gospel-culture.org.uk.

26. Jeremy Begbie (ed.), *Beholding the Glory: incarnation through the arts* (Darton, Longman & Todd, London, 2000), p. xiii.

27. David L. Schindler (ed.), *Catholicism and Secularization in America: essays on nature, grace, and culture* (Communio Books, Notre Dame, 1990). Quotation from p. 12 of Schindler's introduction.

28. *ibid*, pp. 19–20.

29. David Schindler, 'Christological aesthetics and *Evangelium Vitae*: towards a definition of liberalism', *Communio* (Vol. 22, 1995), 198–9.

30. *ibid.*, pp. 215, 217.

31. Schindler, 'Faith and the logic of intelligence: secularization and the academy' in *Catholicism and Secularization in America*, p. 175.

32. Schindler, *art. cit.* (1995), pp. 223–4.

33. Schindler, *art. cit.* (1995), p. 200.

34. Rowan Williams, *Lost Icons: reflections on cultural bereavement* (T. & T. Clark, Edinburgh, 2000), p. 2. Other page references to this book will be included in parenthesis in the text.

35. See David Tracy, 'The uneasy alliance reconceived: Catholic theological method, modernity, and postmodernity', *Theological Studies* (Vol. 50, 1989), 548–70.

Chapter 8: The Postmodern Situation

1. Thomas Berry, *The Dream of the Earth* (Sierra Club, San Francisco, 1990), p. xi.

2. Zygmunt Bauman, *Intimations of Postmodernity* (Routledge, London, 1992), p. x.

3. Robert Kegan has used the term 'reconstructive' to indicate a postmodern tendency to search for new convergences and connections. He has also argued that few people have arrived at the level of psychological integration capable of coping with postmodern complexity of horizons. See his *In Over Our Heads: the mental demands of modern life* (Harvard University Press, Cambridge, 1994).

4. See Thomas Guarino, 'Postmodernity and five fundamental theological issues', *Theological Studies* (Vol. 57, 1996), 54–89; Graham Ward (ed.), *The Postmodern God* (Blackwell, Oxford, 1997).

5. Anthony Giddens, *The Consequences of Modernity* (Polity Press, Cambridge, 1990), p. 3.

6. See Michael J. Buckley, *At the Origins of Modern Atheism* (Yale University Press, New Haven, 1987).

7. See Charles Taylor, *Sources of the Self: the making of modern identity* (Harvard University Press, Cambridge, 1989).

8. Charles Taylor, *The Ethics of Authenticity* (Harvard University Press, Cambridge, 1991), p. 120.

9. David Tracy, 'Theology and the many faces of postmodernity', *Theology Today* (Vol. 51, 1994), 104–14. Quotations from pp. 104–7.

10. David Tracy, 'The post-modern re-naming of God as incomprehensible and hidden', *Cross Currents* (Vol. 50, 2000), 240–7.

11. Most notable in this respect is Bernard Lonergan's *Method in Theology* (Darton, Longman & Todd, London, 1972), ch. 4.

12. Berry, *The Dream of the Earth*, p. 194.

13. See José Maria Mardones, *Síntomas de un retorno* (Sal Terrae, Santander, 1999); Alejandro Llano, *La nuova sensibilità: il positivo della società postmoderna* (Ares, Milan, 1995).

14. Elizabeth Johnson, 'Between the times: religious life and the postmodern experience of God', *Review for Religious* (Vol. 53, 1994), 6–28. Quotations from pp 18–19.

15. Elaine L. Graham, *Transforming Practice: pastoral theology in an age of uncertainty* (Mowbray, London, 1996), pp. 18, 206.

16. George Steiner, *Real Presences* (Faber, London, 1989), pp. 3, 228.

17. David Walsh, *After Ideology: recovering the spiritual foundations of freedom* (Catholic University of America, Washington DC, 1990), pp. 1–2.

18. Jacques Godbout, *The World of the Gift* (McGill-Queen's University Press, Montreal, 1998), ch. 11 *passim*.

19. Quoted in Tony Jones, *Postmodern Youth Ministry* (Zondervan, Grand Rapids, 2001), p. 115.

Chapter 9: Debates about Inculturation

1. Yves Congar, 'Christianity as faith and as culture', *East Asian Pastoral Review* (1981), 304–18. Quotation from p. 308.

2. Robert J. Schreiter, *Constructing Local Theologies* (SCM Press, London, 1985), p. 29.

3. The initial version of this chapter was adapted from an article of mine entitled 'Inculturation: some theological perspectives', published in *International Review of Mission* (Vol. 85, 1996), 173–80. However, for this second edition of *Clashing Symbols* much fresh material has been added.

4. *Collectanea S. C. Progaganda Fide*, I, p. 42, n. 135.

5. Joseph Ratzinger, 'Christ, faith and the challenge of cultures' [Hong Kong Speech of March 1993], *L'Osservatore Romano* (English edition, 26 April 1995), pp. 5–8. Quotations from p. 6.

6. Cecil McGarry in *What Happened at the African Synod*, ed. C. McGarry (Paulines Publications, Nairobi, 1995), p. 188.

7. Christopher Dawson, *Religion and the Rise of Western Culture* (Sheed & Ward, London, 1950), p. 33.

8. John Paul II, *Catechesi tradendae* (1979), No. 53.

9. *Santo Domingo and Beyond: documents and commentaries from the Fourth General Conference of Latin American Bishops*, ed. Alfred Hennelly (Orbis Books, Maryknoll, NY, 1993), Nos. 253–4, pp. 142–3.

10. A more detailed version of this list will be found in my article on 'Spirituality and inculturation' to appear in the *New SCM Press Dictionary of Spirituality* (forthcoming).

11. Pope John Paul II, Letter founding the Pontifical Council for Culture, 20 March 1982.

12. Mario de França Miranda, *Inculturazione della fede: Un approccio teologico* (Queriniana, Brescia, 2002), p. 134.

13. *L'Osservatore Romano*, 27 April 1979.

14. The English text of *Ecclesia in Africa* was published in *L'Osservatore Romano*, English weekly edition, 20 September 1995, as well as in a separate booklet from the Vatican Press. Reference to paragraphs of this document will be given in parenthesis in the text.

15. Mario de França Miranda, *op.cit.*, p. 127.

16. The encyclical *Redemptoris Missio*, No. 54.

17. Jerome Aixala (ed.), *Jesuit Apostolates Today* (Institute of Jesuit Sources, St Louis, 1981), p. 173.

18. Karl Rahner, *Belief Today* (Sheed & Ward, London, 1973), pp. 48–51.

19. Peter C. Phan, 'Cultural diversity: a blessing or a curse for theology and spirituality?', *Louvain Studies* (Vol. 19, 1994), 195–211. References to pp. 201–2.

20. Aylward Shorter, *Toward a Theology of Inculturation* (Geoffrey Chapman, London, 1988), pp. 11–12.

21. Speech to Catechetics Congress, 26 September 1992.

22. 'Our Mission and Culture', No. 22, *Documents of the 34th General Congregation of the Society of Jesus* (Institute of Jesuit Sources, St Louis, 1995), p. 60.

23. Aylward Shorter, *Evangelization and Culture* (Geoffrey Chapman, London, 1994), p. 32.

24. Justin Ukpong, 'Towards a renewed approach to inculturation theology', *Journal of Inculturation Theology* (Vol. 1, 1994), 8–24. Quotation from p. 12.

25. Xolili Keteyi, *Inculturation as a Strategy for Liberation* (Pietermaritzburg, 1998), pp. 21–2.

26. Gerald A. Arbuckle, *From Chaos to Mission: refounding religious life formation* (Geoffrey Chapman, London, 1996), p. 37.

Chapter 10: Cultural Discernment

1. Margaret Archer, *Culture and Agency: the place of culture in social theory* (Cambridge University Press, Cambridge, 1988), p. xxii.

2. Tony Kelly, *Consuming Passions: Christianity and the Consumer Society* (Australian Catholic Bishops Conference, Sydney, 1995), p. 11.

3. Michael Paul Gallagher, *Help my Unbelief*, revised edition (Veritas, Dublin, 1987), p. 46.

4. Josep Vives, 'Dios en el crepusculo del siglo XX', *Razón y Fe* (Vol. 223, 1991), 467–79. Quotation from p. 468. [The play on words exists also in Spanish: 'Falta Dios pero no se le echa en falta'.]

5. James McAuley, 'A letter to John Dryden' in *Anthology of Australian Religious Poetry*, ed. Les Murray (Collins Dove, North Blackburn, 1991), p. 168.

6. This echoes the insights of Stephen Carter, already cited in the Introduction.

7. Anton Houtepen, *God: an open question* (Continuum, London, 2002), pp. 1–3.

8. *Jesus Christ the Bearer of the Water of Life: a Christian reflection on the 'New Age'* (Pontifical Councils for Culture and for Interreligious Dialogue, Vatican City, 2003), p. 12.

9. William Barry, 'U.S. culture and contemporary spirituality', *Review for Religious* (Vol. 54, 1995), 7.

10. Rafael Esteban, 'Evangelization, culture and spirituality', *The Way* (Vol. 34, 1994), 274–5.

11. J. H. Newman, *Grammar of Assent* (Longman, London, 1901), pp. 92–3.

12. T. S. Eliot, *On Poetry and Poets* (Faber & Faber, London, 1957), p. 25.

13. Andrew Greeley, *Religion: a secular theory* (New York, 1982), p. 48. See also his more recent book, *Religion and Poetry* (Transaction Publishers, New York, 1995).

14. H. Richard Niebuhr, *Christ and Culture* (Harper, New York, 1956).

15. Stanley Hauerwas and William Willimon, *Resident Aliens* (Abingdon Press, Nashville, 1991), pp. 30, 145.

16. *The Hauerwas Reader*, ed. J. Berkman and M. Cartwright (Duke University Press, Durham, 2001), p. 585.

17. Speech of 1 October 1962, in *The Documents of Vatican II*, ed. Walter Abbott (Geoffrey Chapman, London, 1966), p. 712.

18. Seamus Murphy, '*Evangelii nuntiandi* twenty years after: culture, pluralism and secularism', *Milltown Studies* (No. 37, Spring 1996), 82–107. Quotation from p. 84.

19. See Ph. Bossuyt and J. Rademakers, 'Rencontre de l'Incroyant et inculturation: Paul à Athenes (Ac. 17, 16–34)', *Nouvelle Revue Théologique* (CXVII, 1995), 19–43.

20. Charles Taylor, *The Ethics of Authenticity* (Harvard University Press, Cambridge, 1991), p. 94.

21. *A Catholic Modernity? Charles Taylor's Marianist Award Lecture*, ed. James Heft (Oxford University Press, New York, 1999), p. 36.

22. 'Our mission and culture' (No. 9), *Documents of the 34th General Congregation of the Society of Jesus* (Institute of Jesuit Sources, St Louis, 1995), p. 54.

Chapter 11: Cultural Consciousness in Faith Ministry

1. Michael Warren, *At This Time in This Place: the Spirit embodied in the local assembly* (Temple Press International, Harrisburg, 1999), p. 1.

2. Riccardo Tonelli, unpublished paper on youth ministry, given at a European Symposium in Rome, May 1994 (my translation).

3. Douglas V. Porpora, *Landscapes of the Soul: the loss of moral meaning in American life* (Oxford University Press, New York, 2001), pp. 10, 209.

4. Douglas Coupland, *Girlfriend in a Coma* (Regan Books, New York, 1998), pp. 165, 259, 264, 284.

5. Douglas Coupland, *Life after God* (Pocket Books, New York, 1995), pp. 359–60.

6. Thomas Beaudoin, *Virtual Faith: the irreverent spiritual quest of generation X* (Jossey-Bass Inc., San Francisco, 1998), pp. 177–8.

7. Interview with Massimo Cacciari, *La Repubblica* (Rome newspaper), 17.1.03.

8. Michael Budde, *The (Magic) Kingdom of God: Christianity and global culture industries* (Westview, Boulder, 1997), pp. 99, 124.

9. Quoted by Michael Warren, *Faith, Culture and the Worshipping Community*, revised edition (Pastoral Press, Washington DC, 1993), p. 160.

10. Michael Warren, *Youth, Gospel, Liberation*, 2nd edition (Don Bosco Multimedia, New Rochelle, 1994), p. 143.

11. John F. Kavanaugh, *Following Christ in a Consumer Society: the spirituality of cultural resistance*, revised edition (Orbis Books, New York, 1991), p. 21.

12. *ibid*, p. 113.

13. John Kavanaugh, 'Five moral crises', *America* (6–13 January 2003), 24.

14. Michael Warren, *Communications and Cultural Analysis* (Bergin & Garvey, Westport, Conn., 1992), p. 118. This book has been republished with the title *Seeing through the Media* – see Bibliography.

15. Kavanaugh, *Following Christ*, p. 165.

16. Michael Warren, 'The material conditions of our seeing and perceiving', *New Theology Review* (Vol. 7, 1994), 37–59, Quotation from.p. 57.

17. Michael Warren, 'Catechesis and (or) religious education' in *Religious Education as Practical Theology*, ed. B. Roebben and M. Warren (Peeters, Leuven, 2001), p. 143.
18. Warren, *Communications and Cultural Analysis*, pp. 6, 16.
19. Warren, *At This Time in This Place*, p. 12.
20. Michael Warren, *Faith, Culture and the Worshipping Community* (Paulist Press, New York, 1989), p. xii.
21. Kavanaugh, *Following Christ*, p. 162.
22. Warren, *Youth, Gospel, Liberation*, p. 152.
23. Warren, *Communications and Cultural Analysis*, pp. 8–9.
24. Kavanaugh, *Following Christ*, p. 127.
25. Warren, *Communications and Cultural Analysis*, p. 13.
26. Warren, *Gospel, Youth, Liberation*, p. 153.
27. Ludwig Wittgenstein, *Culture and Value*, ed. G. H. von Wright (Blackwell, Oxford, 1980), p. 64.
28. Kavanaugh, *Following Christ*, p. 137.
29. John F. Kavanaugh, *Who Counts as Persons? human identity and the ethics of killing* (Georgetown University Press, Washington DC, 2001), pp. 105, 56.

Chapter 12: *Towards a Spirituality of Culture*

1. Veronica Brady, 'Postmodernism and the spiritual life', *The Way* (Vol. 36, 1996), 179.
2. Quoted in Konrad Raiser, *For a Culture of Life: transforming globalization and violence* (WCC Publications, Geneva, 2002), p. 152.
3. Seamus Heaney, *Station Island* (Faber & Faber, London, 1984), p. 118. It seems appropriate to begin this final chapter with a text from 'creative culture'. This artistic dimension has been somewhat neglected in this book because of the vastly increased attention given to 'lived culture' in recent years in religious and theological circles. However, since the first edition of *Clashing Symbols*, I have published *Dive Deeper: the human poetry of faith* (Darton, Longman & Todd, London, 2001) in which I draw on the riches of literature to evoke thresholds of spirituality.
4. This expression was first used by John Paul II in Port-au-Prince, 3 March 1983.
5. J. R. R. Tolkien, *Tree and Leaf* (Unwin, London, 1964), pp. 60–2.
6. See Donal Dorr, *Divine Energy* (Gill and Macmillan, Dublin, 1996).
7. The quoted phrases here come from Charles Taylor, 'Spirituality of life – and its shadow', *Compass* (Toronto, May–June 1996), 12.
8. Sandra Schneiders, 'Spirituality in the academy', *Theological Studies* (Vol. 50, 1989), 684.

9. Philip Sheldrake, *Spirituality and History* (SPCK, London, 1991), pp. 37, 52.

10. Thomas Moore, *The Soul's Religion: cultivating a profoundly spiritual way of life* (Harper Collins, New York, 2002), pp. 97, 242–3.

11. Michael Kearney, *Mortally Wounded: stories of soul pain, death and healing* (Marino Books, Dublin, 1996), pp. 60, 63. These insights from a consultant in palliative medicine, writing mainly about therapy with the terminally ill, are also applicable to a larger spiritual crisis in our culture. I had the pleasure of discussing this point with Dr Kearney, who was in agreement with this broadening of the agenda from the personal to the cultural.

12. See my article 'Apologetics: towards a different agenda', *Priests and People* (Vol. 9, 1995), 367–71.

13. Vaclav Havel, 'Postmodern world needs new principle' [Philadelphia Speech], *Arizona Daily Star*, 8 July 1994.

14. William D. Dinges, 'Postmodernism and religious institutions', *The Way* (Vol. 36, 1996), 218–19.

15. James Bacik, *Spirituality in Transition* (Sheed & Ward, Kansas, 1996), pp. 22, 31, 43–5, 49.

16. Ronald Rolheiser, *The Shattered Lantern* (Hodder & Stoughton, London, 1994), p. 45.

17. Pierangelo Sequeri, *Sensibili allo Spirito: Umanesimo religioso e ordine degli affetti* (Glossa, Milan, 2001), p. 13.

18. Hans Urs von Balthasar with Angelo Scola, *Test Everything: hold fast to what is good* (Ignatius Press, San Francisco, 1989), pp. 25–6, 50, 52.

Epilogue: Roots and Horizons

1. Letter of 1843, quoted in Ian Ker, *John Henry Newman: a biography* (Oxford University Press, Oxford, 1988), p. 273.

2. Mary Oliver, *Blue Pastures* (Harvest Books, New York, 1995), p. 117.

3. See the eloquent argument on community and family by Jonathan Sacks in his book *Faith in the Future* (Darton, Longman & Todd, London, 1994).

4. See Robert Doran, *Theology and the Dialectics of History* (University of Toronto Press, Toronto, 1990), p. 134.

5. Bernard Lonergan, *A Third Collection*, ed. F. E. Crowe (Geoffrey Chapman, London, 1985), p. 158.

Select Bibliography

Arbuckle, Gerald A., *Earthing the Gospel: an inculturation handbook for pastoral workers* (Geoffrey Chapman, London, 1990).

——, *Refounding the Church* (Geoffrey Chapman, London, 1993).

——, *From Chaos to Mission: refounding religious life formation* (Geoffrey Chapman, London, 1996).

Ariarajah, S. Wesley, *Gospel and Culture: an ongoing discussion within the Ecumenical Movement* (Gospel and Cultures Pamphlet 1, WCC Publications, Geneva, 1994).

Barry, William, 'U.S. culture and contemporary spirituality', *Review for Religious* (Vol. 54, 1995), 6–21.

Berger, Peter, ed., *The Desecularization of the World: resurgent religion and world politics* (Eerdmans, Grand Rapids, 1999).

Berry, Thomas, *The Dream of the Earth* (Sierra Club, San Francisco, 1990).

Brady, Veronica, 'Postmodernism and the spiritual life', *The Way* (Vol. 36, 1996), 179–87.

Bruner, Jerome, *The Culture of Education* (Harvard University Press, Cambridge, 1996).

Budde, Michael, *The (Magic) Kingdom of God: Christianity and global culture industries* (Westview, Boulder, 1997).

Carrier, Hervé, *Evangelizing the Culture of Modernity* (Orbis Books, New York, 1993).

Carter, Stephen L., *The Culture of Disbelief: how American law and politics trivialize religious devotion* (Basic Books, New York, 1993).

Casanova, José, *Public Religions in the Modern World* (University of Chicago Press, Chicago, 1994).

Davies, Oliver, *A Theology of Compassion* (SCM Press, London, 2001).

Dawson, Christopher, *Religion and Culture* (Sheed & Ward, London, 1948).

Douglas, Mary, *Natural Symbols: explorations in cosmology* (Cresset Press, London, 1970).

——, *Risk and Blame: essays in cultural theory* (Routledge, London, 1992).

——, *In the Wilderness* (Academic Press, Sheffield, 1993).

Dupré, Louis, *Passage to Modernity* (Yale University Press, New Haven, 1993).

Duraisingh, Christopher, ed., *Called to One Hope: the gospel in diverse cultures* (WCC Publications, Geneva, 1998).

Eagleton, Terry, *The Idea of Culture* (Blackwell, Oxford, 2000).

Eliot, T. S., *Notes towards the Definition of Culture* (Faber & Faber, London, 1948).

Esteban, Rafael, 'Evangelization, Culture and Spirituality', *The Way* (Vol. 34, 1994), 273–82.

Flanagan, Kieran, *The Enchantment of Sociology: a study of theology and culture* (Macmillan, London, 1996).

Gallagher, Michael Paul, *What Are They Saying about Unbelief?* (Paulist, New York, 1995).

——, 'From social to cultural secularization', *Louvain Studies* (Vol. 24, 1999), 103–18.

——, *Dive Deeper: the human poetry of faith* (Darton, Longman & Todd, London, 2001).

Geertz, Clifford, *The Interpretation of Cultures* (Basic Books, New York, 1973).

Giddens, Anthony, *The Consequences of Modernity* (Polity Press, Cambridge, 1990).

Girard, René, *The Girard Reader*, ed. James Williams (Crossroad, New York, 1997).

Godbout, Jacques, *The World of the Gift* (McGill-Queen's University Press, Montreal, 1998).

Graham, Elaine L., *Transforming Practice: pastoral theology in an age of uncertainty* (Mowbray, London, 1996).

Greeley, Andrew, *Religion and Poetry* (Transaction Publishers, New York, 1995).

Gremillion, Joseph, ed., *The Church and Culture since Vatican II* (University of Notre Dame Press, Notre Dame, 1985).

Guardini, Romano, *The End of the Modern World* (Sheed & Ward, London, 1950).

——, *Letters from Lake Como* (Eerdmans, Grand Rapids, 1994).

Hauerwas, Stanley, *The Hauerwas Reader*, ed. J. Berkman and M. Cartwright (Duke University Press, Durham, 2001).

Houtepen, Anton, *God: an open question* (Continuum, London, 2002).

Huntington, Samuel, 'The clash of civilizations?', *Foreign Affairs* (Summer 1993), 22–49.

Inglis, Fred, *Cultural Studies* (Blackwell, Oxford, 1993).

Johnson, Elizabeth, 'Between the times: religious life and the postmodern experience of God', *Review for Religious* (Vol. 53, 1994), 6–28.

Kavanaugh, John F., *Following Christ in a Consumer Society: the spirituality of cultural resistance*, revised edition (Orbis Books, New York, 1991).

Kearney, Michael, *Mortally Wounded: stories of soul pain, death and healing* (Marino Books, Dublin, 1996).

Kegan, Robert, *In Over Our Heads: the mental demands of modern life* (Harvard University Press, Cambridge, 1994).

Kolakowski, Leszek, *Modernity on Endless Trial* (University of Chicago Press, Chicago, 1990).

Kroeber, A. L. and Kluckhohn, Clyde, *Culture: a critical review of concepts and definitions* (Vintage Books, New York, 1963).

Lakeland, Paul, *Postmodernity: Christian identity in a fragmented age* (Fortress Press, Minneapolis, 1997).

Lane, Dermot, ed., *Religion and Culture in Dialogue* (Columba Press, Dublin, 1993).

Llano, Alejandro, *La nuova sensibilità: il positivo della società postmoderna* (Ares, Milan, 1995).

Lonergan, Bernard, *Insight: a study of human understanding* (Longman Green, London, 1958).

——, *Method in Theology* (Darton, Longman & Todd, London, 1972).

Miguens, Fernando, *Fe y Culture en la Enseñanza de Juan Pablo II* (Ediciones Palabra, Madrid, 1994).

Montefiore, Hugh, ed., *The Gospel and Contemporary Culture* (Mowbray, London, 1992).

Murphy, Seamus, 'Evangelii nuntiandi twenty years after: culture, pluralism and secularism', *Milltown Studies* (No. 37, Spring 1996), 82–107.

Newbigin, Lesslie, *Foolishness to the Greeks* (SPCK, London, 1986).

——, *Gospel in a Pluralist Society* (SPCK, London, 1989).

Niebuhr, H. Richard, *Christ and Culture* (Harper, New York, 1956).

Ong, Walter J., *Orality and Literacy: the technologizing of the word* (Routledge, London, 1982).

——, *Faith and Contexts* [Collected Essays 1952–91], 2 vols, ed. Thomas Farrell (Scholars Press, Atlanta, 1992).

Osborn, Lawrence, *Restoring the Vision: the gospel and modern culture* (Mowbray, London, 1995).

Porpora, Douglas V., *Landscapes of the Soul: the loss of moral meaning in American life* (Oxford University Press, New York, 2001).

Poupard, Paul, *The Church and Culture: challenge and confrontation* (Central Bureau CCVA, St Louis, 1994).

Raiser, Konrad, 'Gospel and cultures', *International Review of Mission* (Vol. 83, No. 331, 1994), 623–9.

——, *For a Culture of Life: transforming globalization and violence* (WCC Publications, Geneva, 2002).

Rolheiser, Ronald, *The Shattered Lantern* (Hodder & Stoughton, London, 1994).

Roest Crollius, Ary, *What Is So New about Inculturation?* (Gregorian University Press, Rome, 1984).

Sacks, Jonathan, *Faith in the Future* (Darton, Longman & Todd, London, 1995).

Schindler, David L., ed., *Catholicism and Secularization in America: essays on nature, grace, and culture* (Communio Books, Notre Dame, 1990).

Schneiders, Sandra, 'Spirituality in the academy', *Theological Studies* (Vol. 50, 1989), 676–97.

Schreiter, Robert J., *Constructing Local Theologies* (SCM Press, London, 1985).

Scruton, Roger, *An Intelligent Person's Guide to Modern Culture* (Duckworth, London, 1998).

Shorter, Aylward, *Towards a Theology of Inculturation* (Geoffrey Chapman, London, 1988).

Swidler, Ann, *Talk of Love: how culture matters* (University of Chicago Press, Chicago, 2001).

Tanner, Kathryn, *Theories of Culture: a new agenda for theology* (Fortress Press, Minneapolis, 1997).

Taylor, Charles, *Sources of the Self: the making of modern identity* (Harvard University Press, Cambridge, 1989).

——, *The Ethics of Authenticity* (Harvard University Press, Cambridge, 1991).

——, *A Catholic Modernity? Marianist Award Lecture*, ed. James Heft (Oxford University Press, New York, 1999).

Touraine, Alain, *Critique of Modernity* (Blackwell, Oxford, 1995).

Tracy, David, 'Theology and the many faces of postmodernity', *Theology Today* (Vol. 51, 1994), 104–14.

——, 'The post-modern re-naming of God as incomprehensible and hidden', *Cross Currents* (Vol. 50, 2000), 240–7.

Walsh, David, *The Third Millennium: reflections on faith and reason* (Georgetown University Press, Washington, 1999).

Warren, Michael, *At This Time in This Place: the spirit embodied in the local assembly* (Temple Press International, Harrisburg, 1999).

——, *Seeing through the Media* (Trinity Press, Harrisburg, 1997).

——, *Youth, Gospel, Liberation*, second edition (Don Bosco Multimedia, New Rochelle, 1994).

Williams, Raymond, *Culture* (Fontana, London, 1981).

——, *Culture and Society* (Hogarth Press, London, 1993).

——, *The Long Revolution* (Chatto & Windus, London, 1961).

Williams, Rowan, *Lost Icons: reflections on cultural bereavement* (T. & T. Clark, Edinburgh, 2000).

Wojtyla, Karol, *Person and Community: selected essays*, tr. Theresa Sandok (Peter Lang, New York, 1993).

Wuthnow, Robert, *Christianity in the Twenty-first Century* (Oxford University Press, Oxford, 1993).

Yuhaus, Cassian, ed., *The Catholic Church and American Culture* (Paulist Press, New York, 1990).